Rough, unkept, spontaneous and free, Grzegorz Wróblewski's *Shanty Town* depicts a blurry world of post-literate indecipherability. With coarsely drawn shapes imposed upon a chaos of asemic writing, this collection is built from the rubble of uncomfortable truths. A triumph of bold writing.

— **Dave Read**

Shanty Town packs a powerful punch. It stakes you straight through the heart and throws you overboard, only to next moment toss you a life buoy. It's Grzegorz Wróblewski's opus magnum, in which he brought together the heart and the mind on a whole new level. I see a world that worries him but nonetheless he manages to draw pure beauty from it. Somewhere in between, a fragile hope for salvation emerges. His own and ours.

— **Karina Obara**

Manic notes from the underbelly. Scores scored out and scorching. Fenced off communities of frozen language. Prisons, pens and penal markings. Lines are blocked off, squashed into huddles and forever ringed or scarred. Sometimes a shape emerges shaken, tries to connect, map and communicate the inner terrain; but there's pain and great beauty here we can barely contemplate. Grzegorz Wróblewski's writings express the world village in trauma. There's nothing left to say, and this is the only way of saying it.

— **Stephen Nelson**

The asemic projects of Grzegorz Wróblewski are a testimony to the skills of the human hand, used to convey meaning over millennia of evolution. In the infinite repetition of shapes, lines and colors, the hand reaches a state of maximum sensitivity that allows it to detect the epiphanic proto-signals of the micro- and macroworld.

—**Anna Matysiak**

Shanty Town is an unusual work, full of compositions unlike anything else I've seen. The pages appear to have been made in 2 stages, drawn annotations over handwritten or hand-drawn ideas underneath. The first stage ranges from well-behaved written lines as in a letter, to jerky scribbled fragmentary jottings, to sketchy doodles, young ideas captured at high speed. The second stage uses shapes such as rectangles, circles and lines, which appear to be organizing or explaining the first stage they partly cover. Although rectangles and rectangular frames are widely used, these works are at the loosest end of rectilinearity. Wróblewski uses visual rhetoric in a poetic way.

—**Tim Gaze**, author of *Glyphs of Uncertain Meaning*, publisher of *Asemic* magazine

Shanty Town

Grzegorz Wróblewski

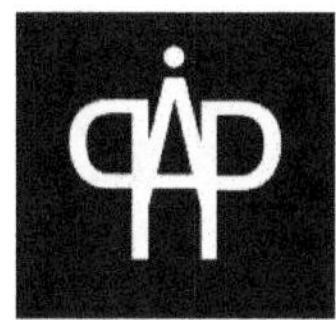

Post-Asemic Press 019

ISBN-13: 978-1-7348662-7-8

Contact: postasemicpress@gmail.com

Postasemicpress.wordpress.com

Postasemicpress.blogspot.com

Cover design by Grzegorz Wróblewski &

Michael Jacobson

An introduction to *Shanty Town*

This is not a dog although the natives describe him as such

he must have fallen out of the sky

I have a small painting by Grzegorz Wróblewski hanging above the doorway to what was once a verandah around part of the upper story of our house but which, before our time here, was blown in during a cyclone & is now enclosed & serves as my study. The painting is primarily yellow, & has shapes in it which can be read as a dog, onlookers, a central figure.

There are other shapes in the painting, abstract, open. Their designation is unclear, but it is obvious that they are important to the entirety of the piece. Here the focus is on the larger shapes; in later paintings the smaller shapes become more prevalent, increase in size, while the 'recognizable' shapes become smaller & are often reduced to angular cartoon heads. The two variants share the space on an equal footing.

Shanty Town shares its space between writing in an unknown & unrecognizable language & an overlay of shapes, some similar to those in earlier paintings, others of a rough geometric nature — circles, rectangles. The shapes are given prominence by the weight of their outlines, but these could equally be considered highlighters, so the writing challenges them for supremacy because of the extent of it. Put them all together, & it is reinforcement that Grzegorz Wróblewski has always been both artist & writer.

He considers each living being to be a separate cosmos, but all are residents of a community called Shanty Town, positioned at the edge of the world &, because of the contiguity, therefore the edge of space as well. In *Shanty Town* he is our singular & collective voice, a man who "wants to leave a message to the future inhabitants of Earth."

The individual pieces in *Shanty Town* have a kind of religious majesty to them, but they are basic, not polished or stylized like icons or stained glass windows. They appear as the bare bones of belief, personal & personalized but still accessible to all, in a common language.

" Let everyone find themselves or a dream about themselves in this book. The interpretation is open."

—Mark Young, editor at ***Otoliths***

Shanty Town

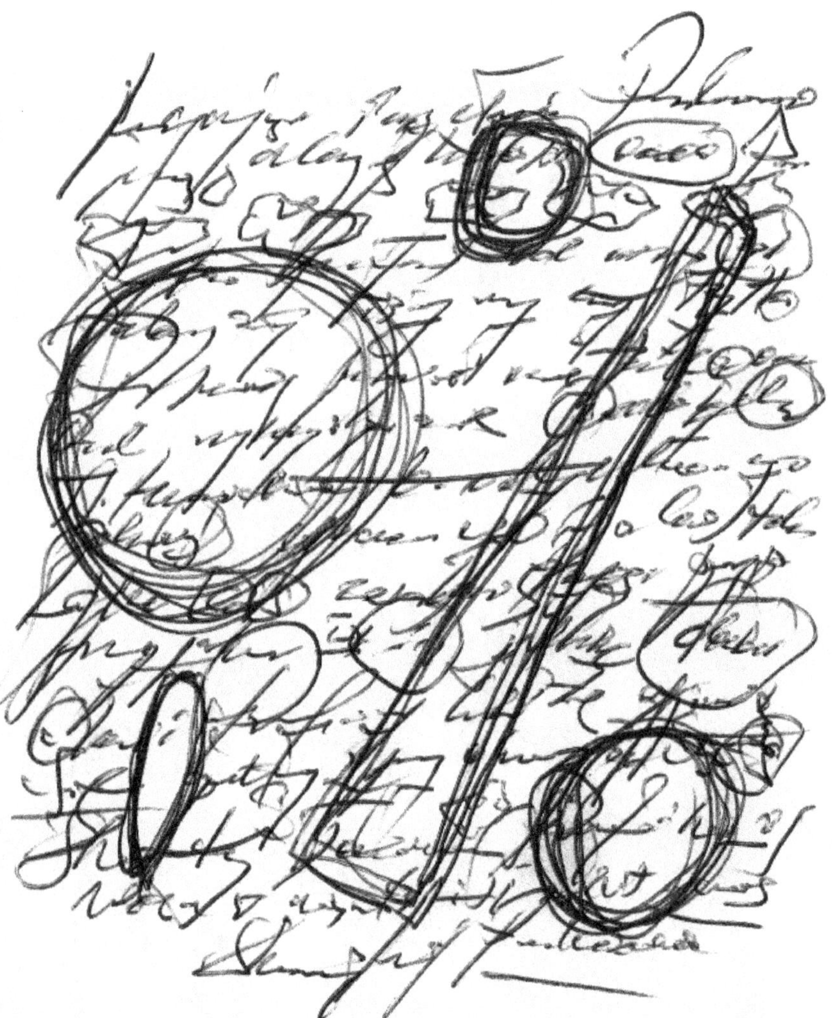

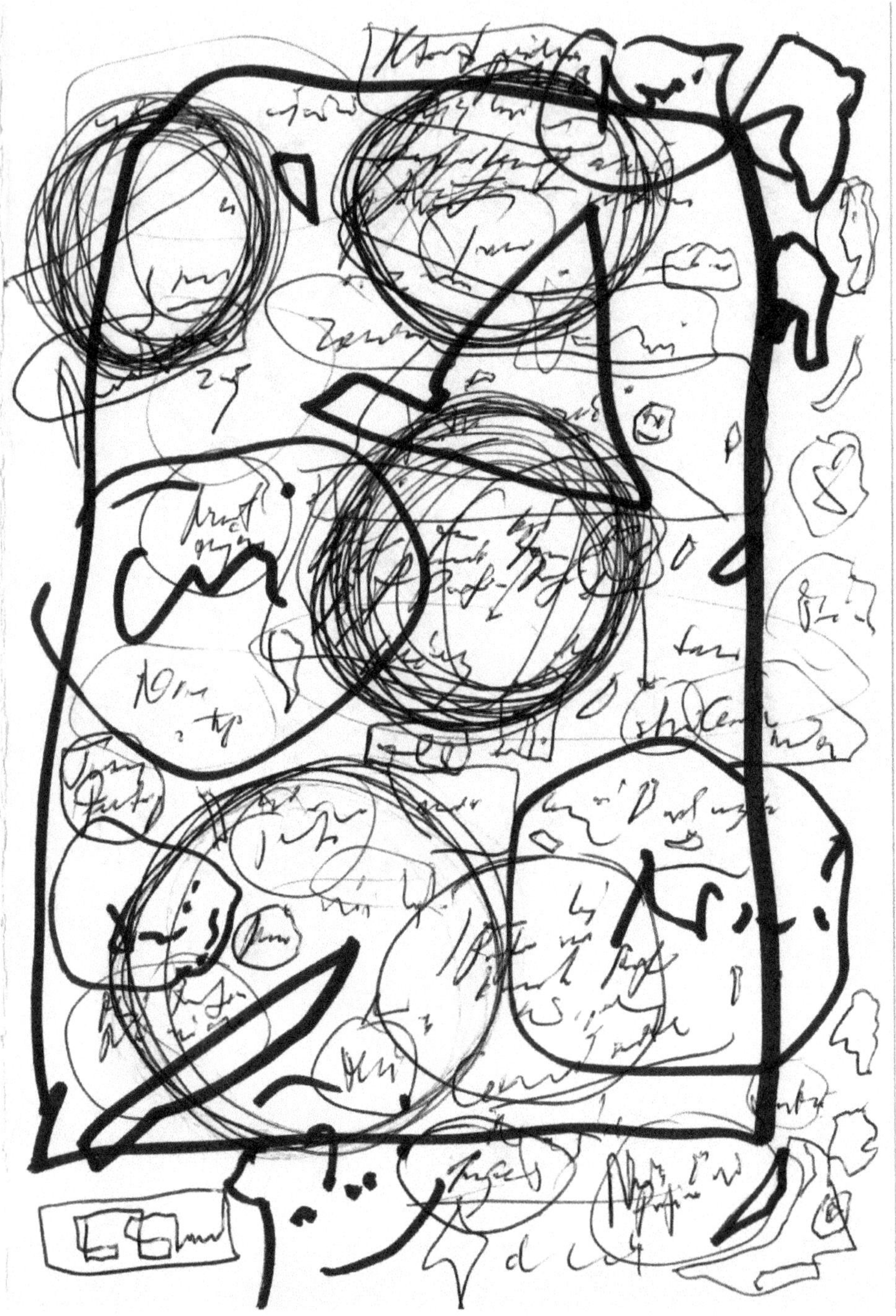

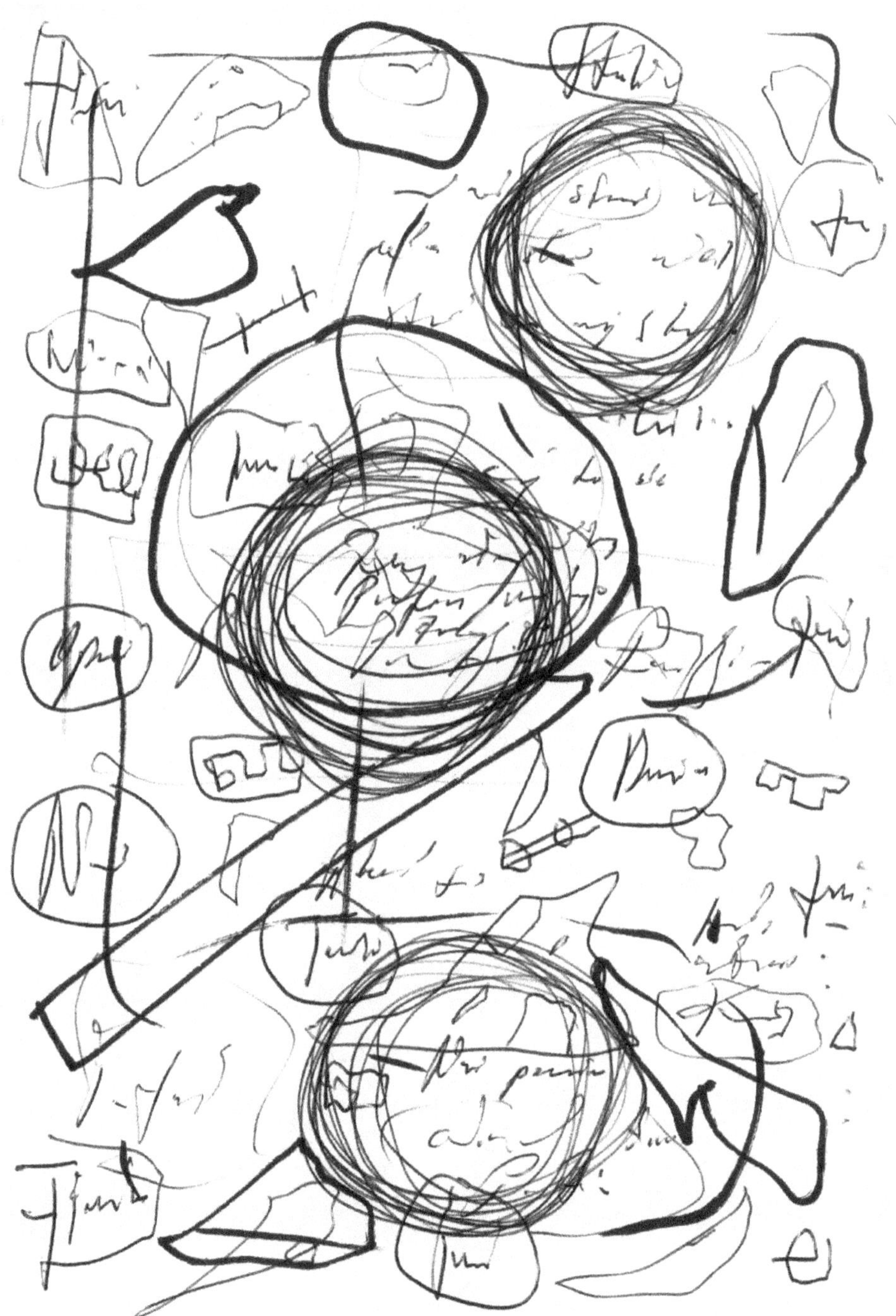

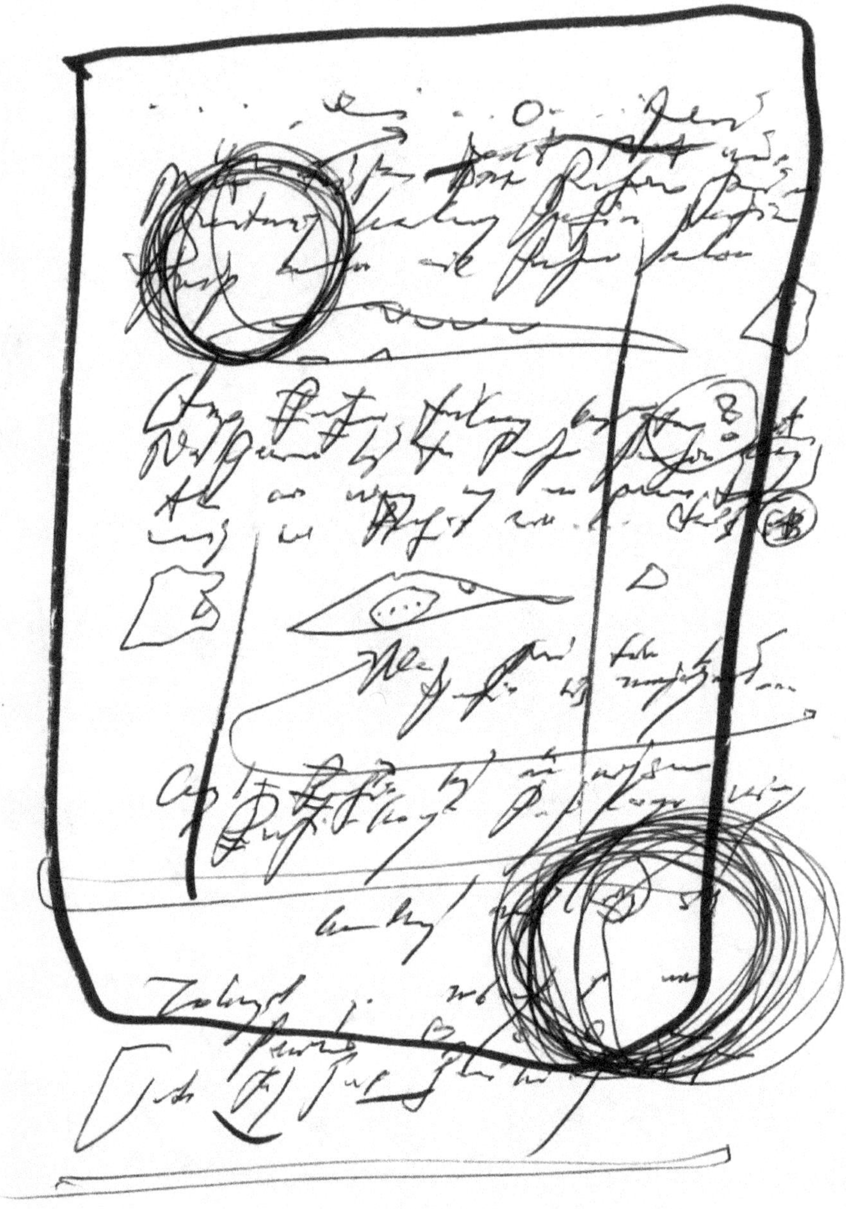

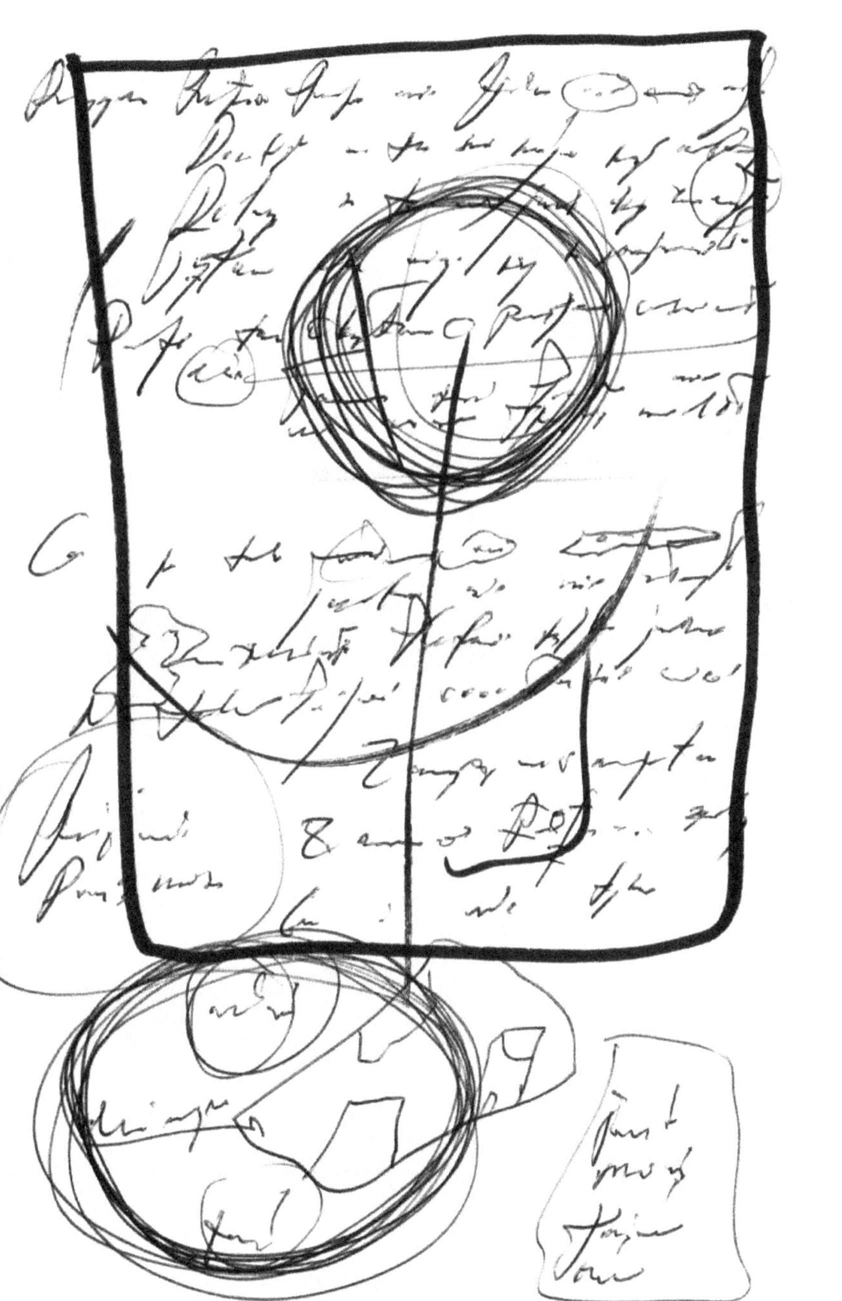

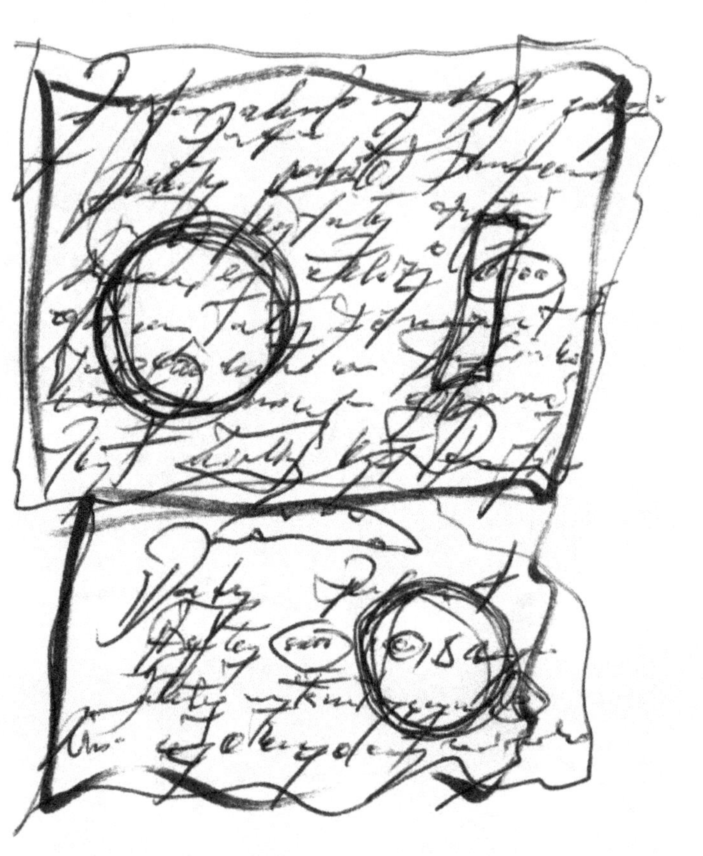

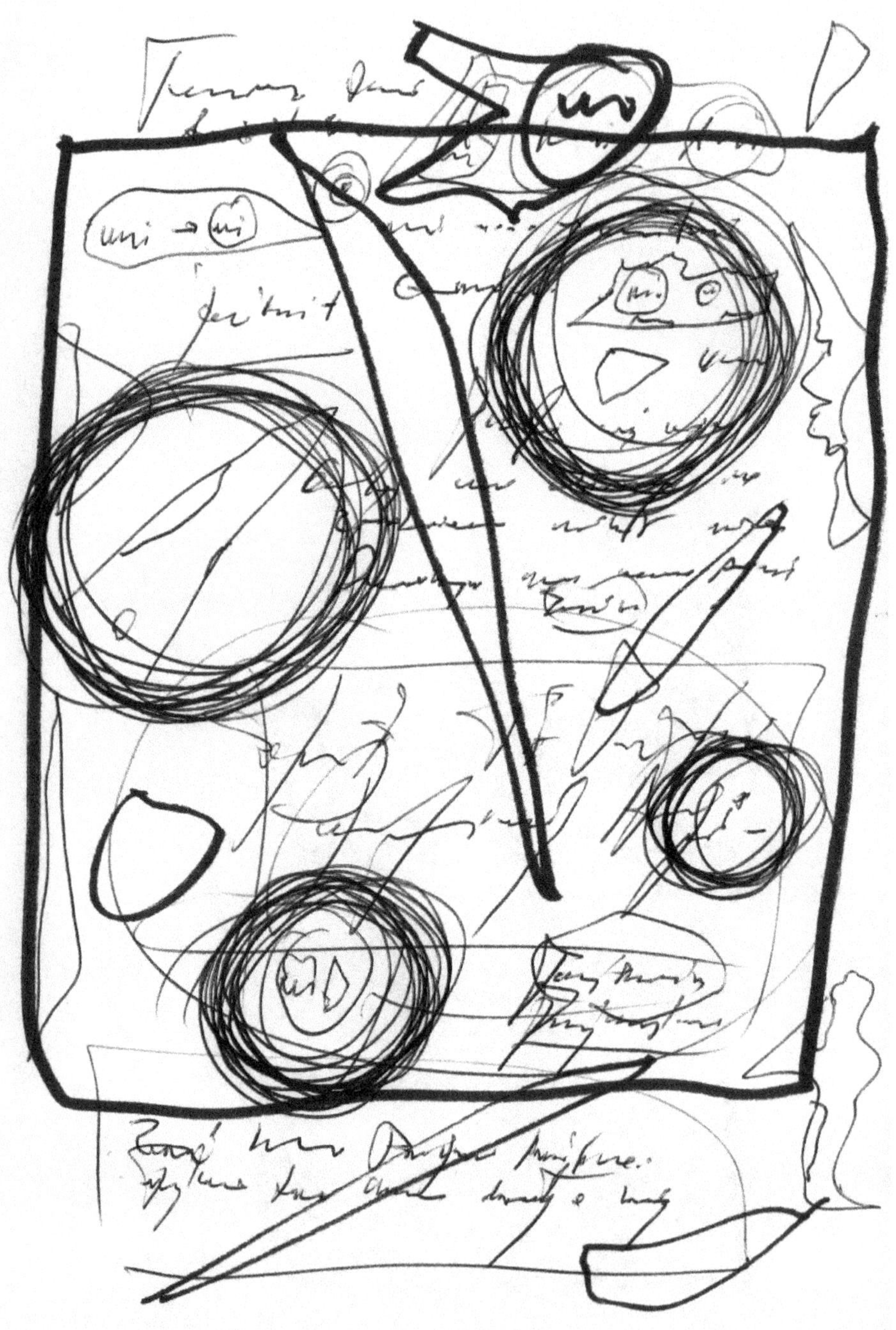

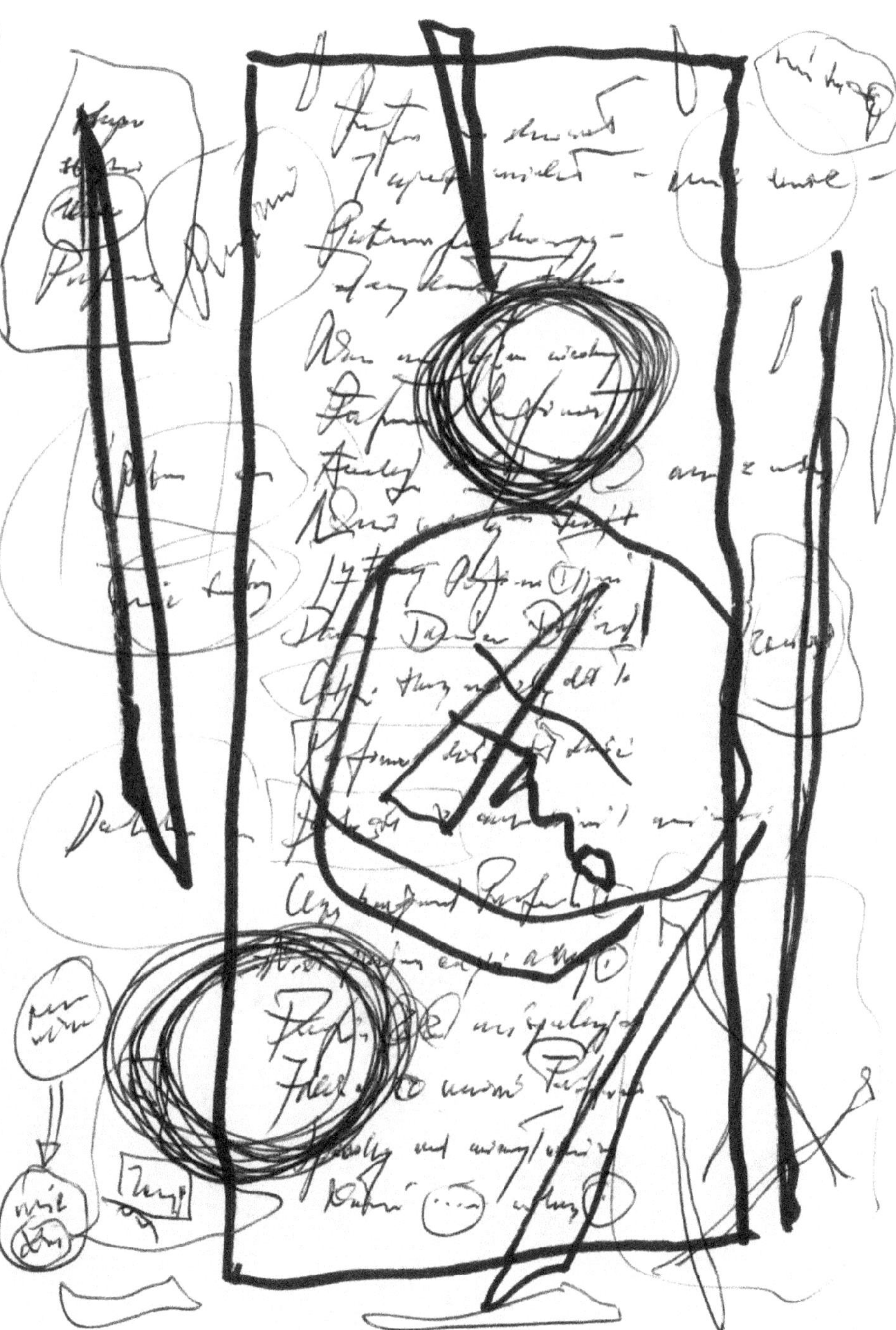

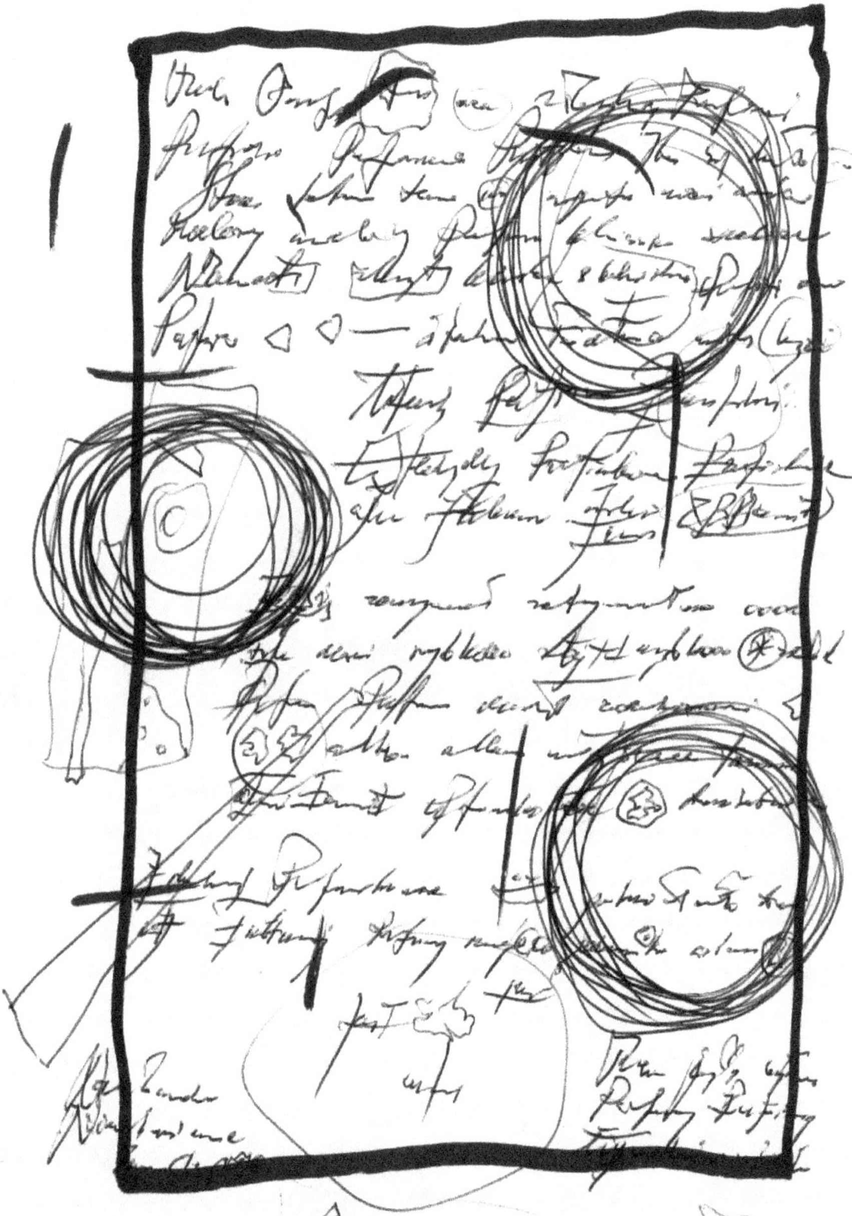

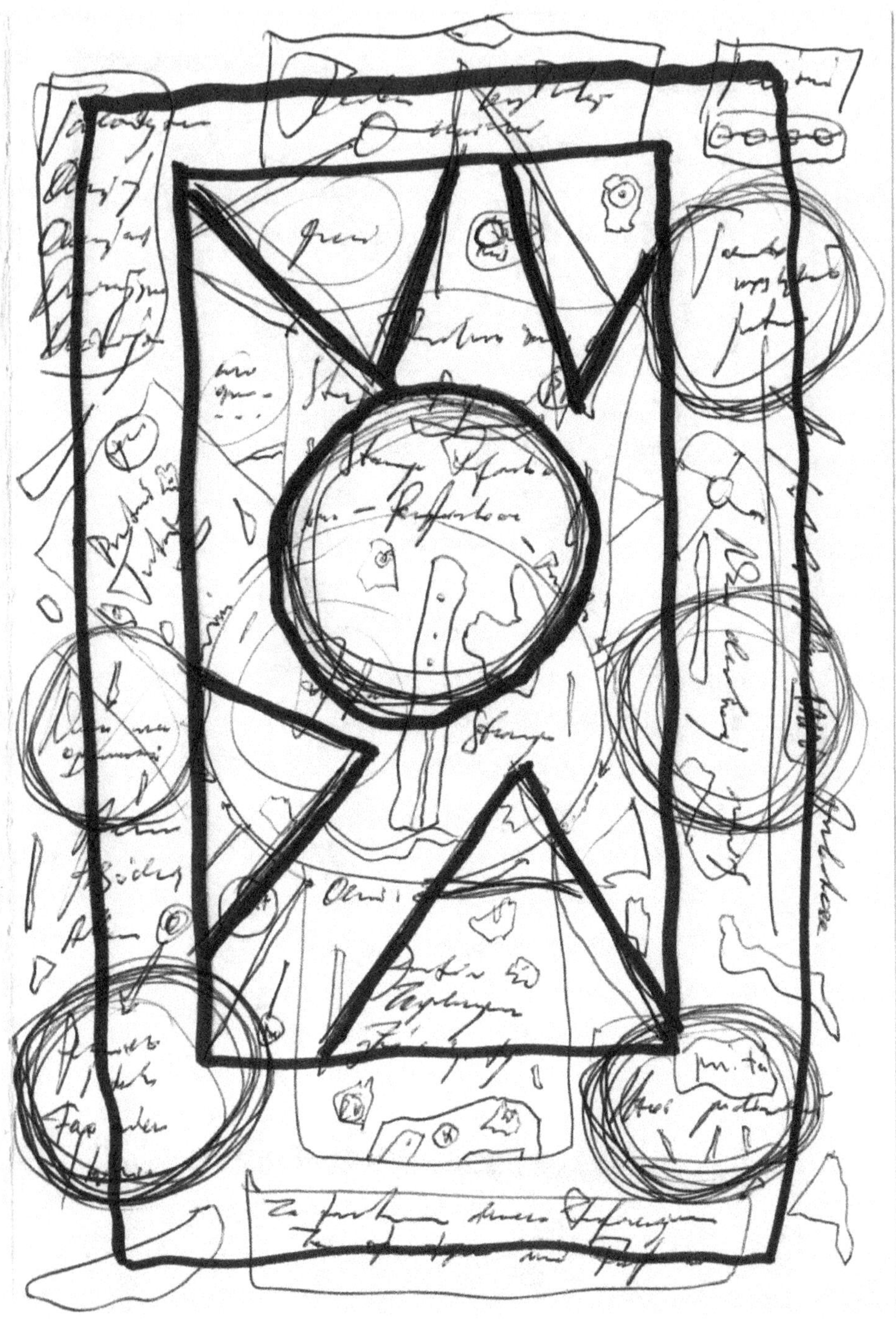

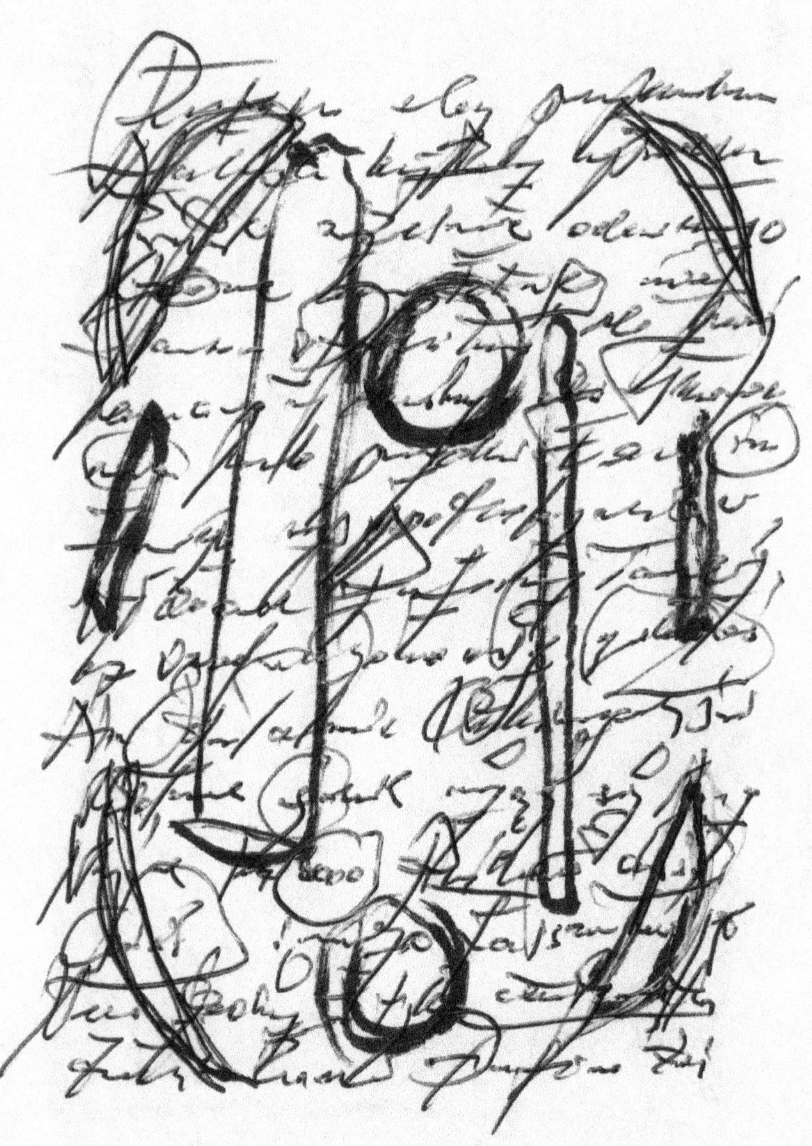

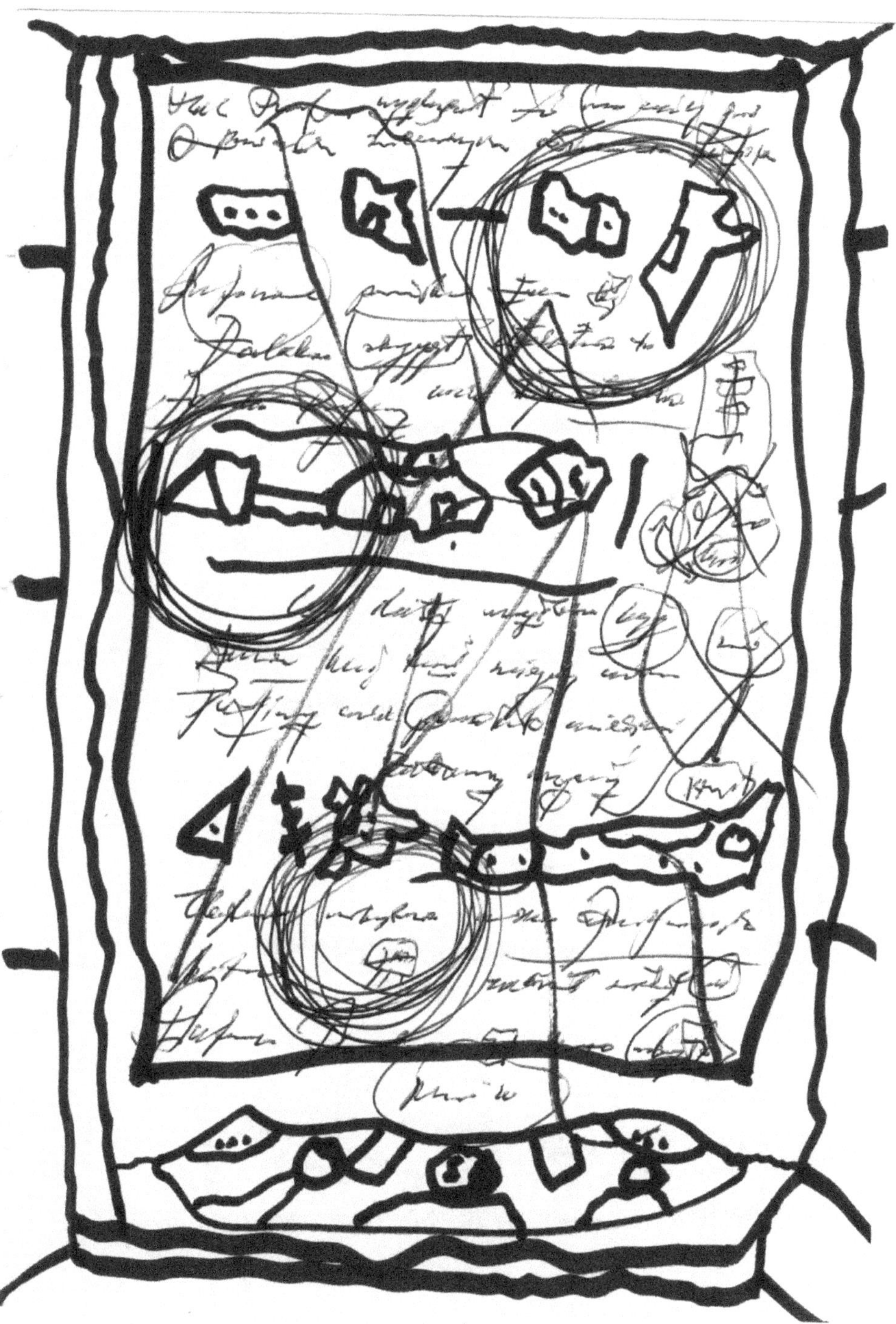

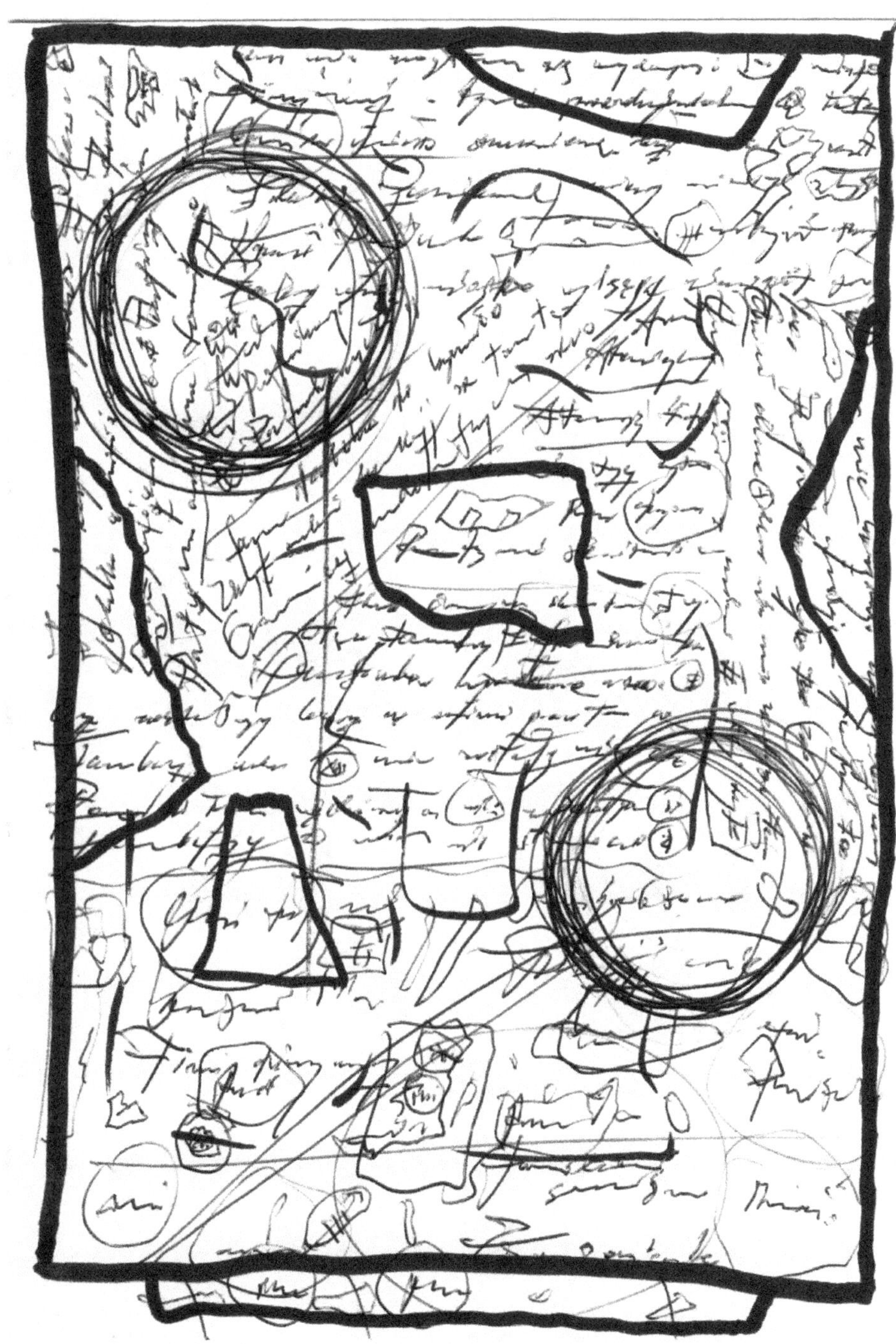

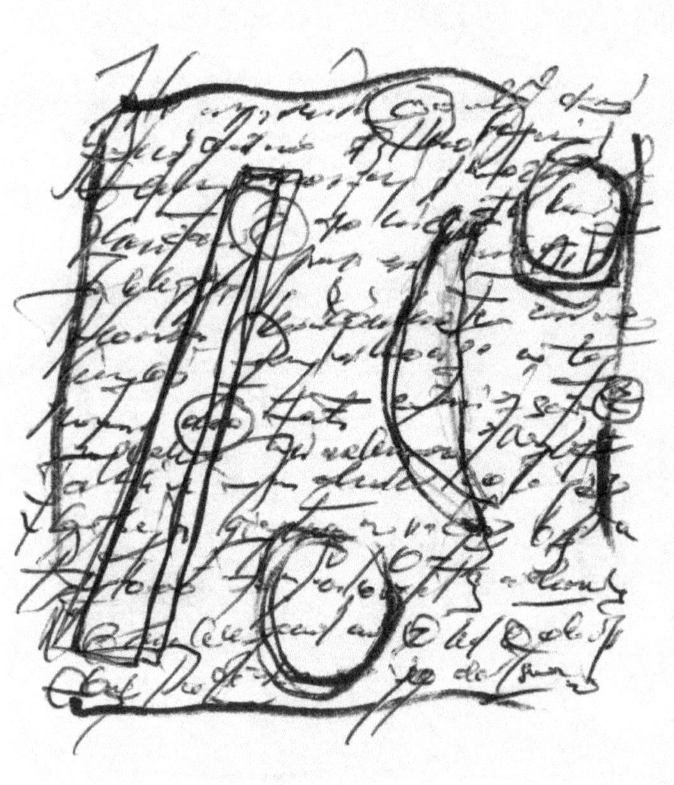

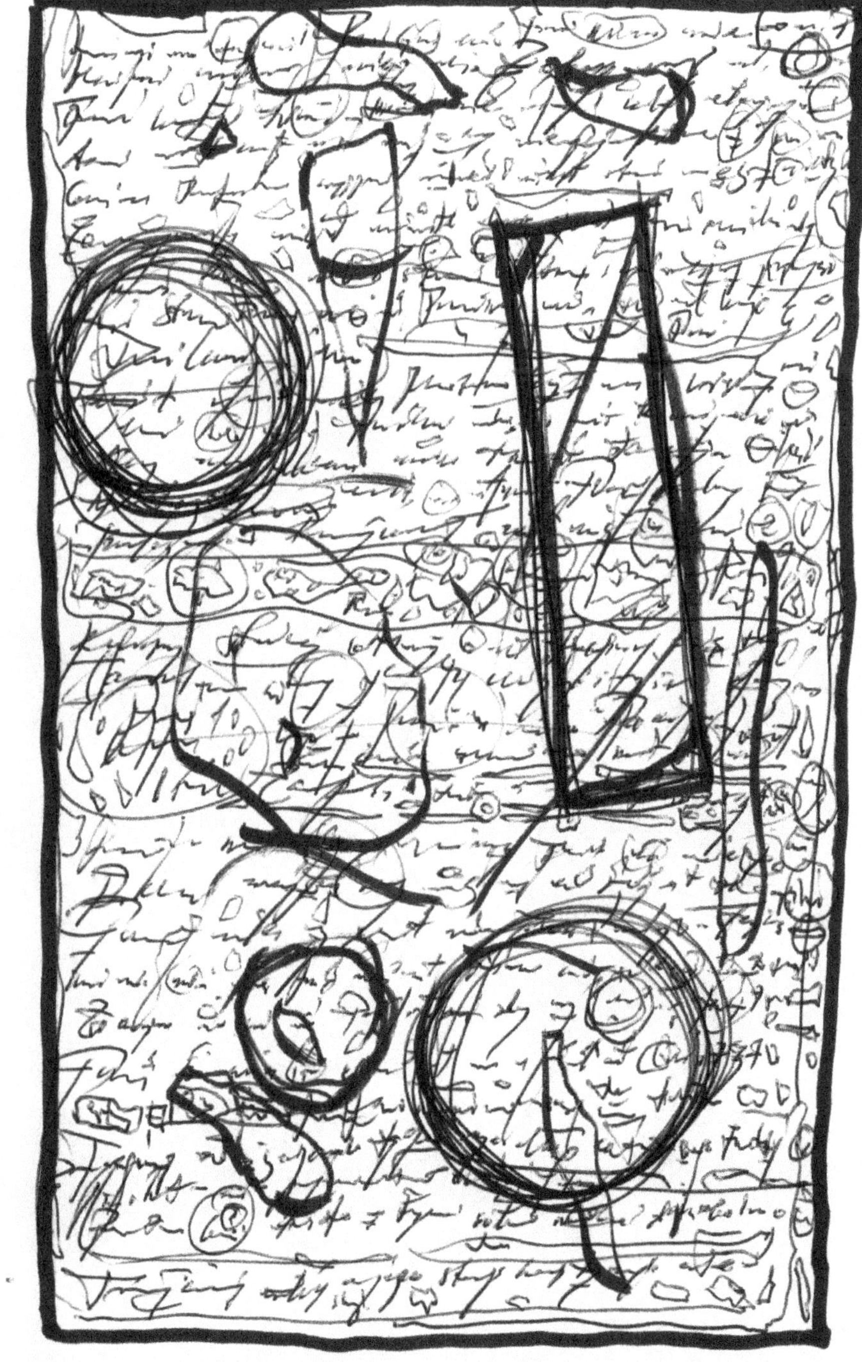

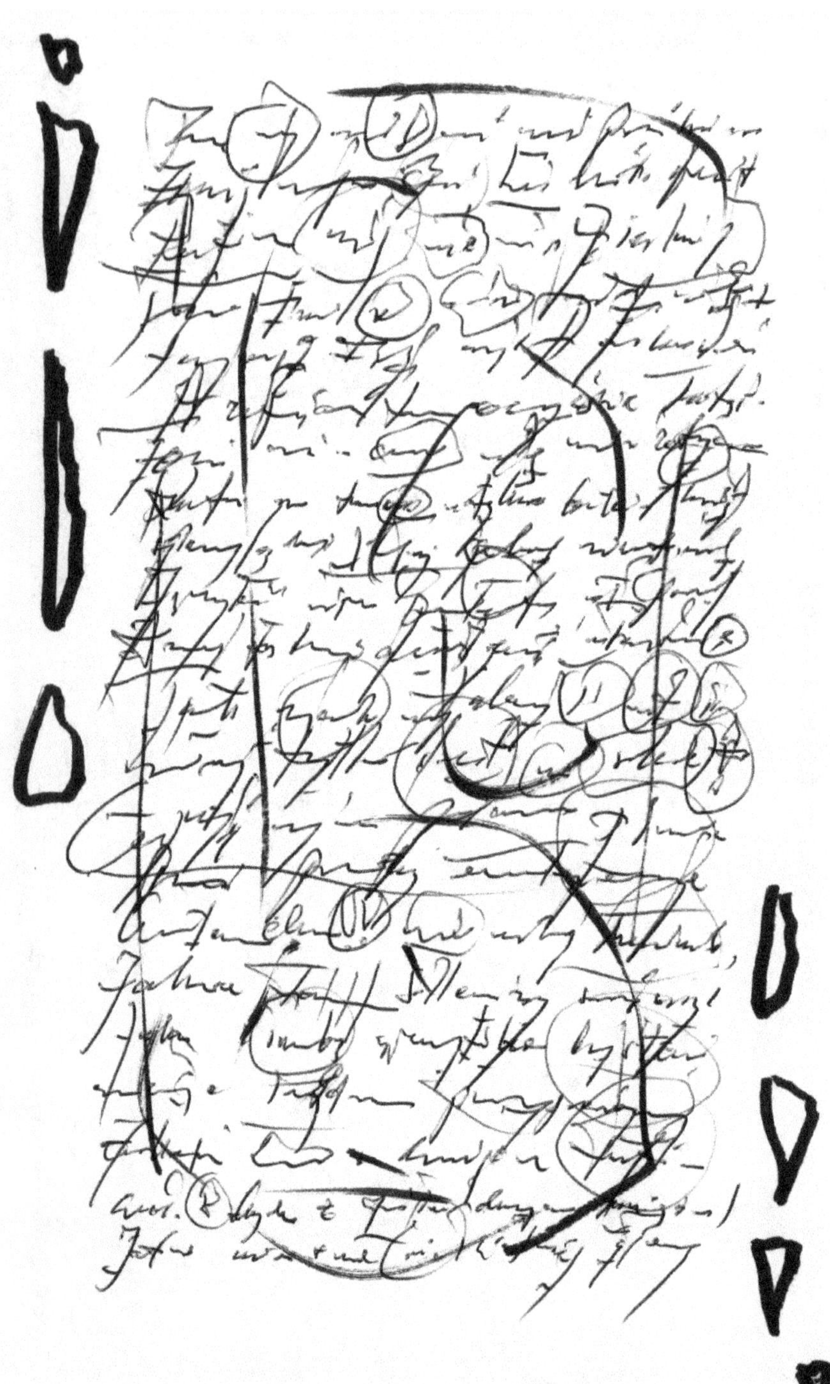

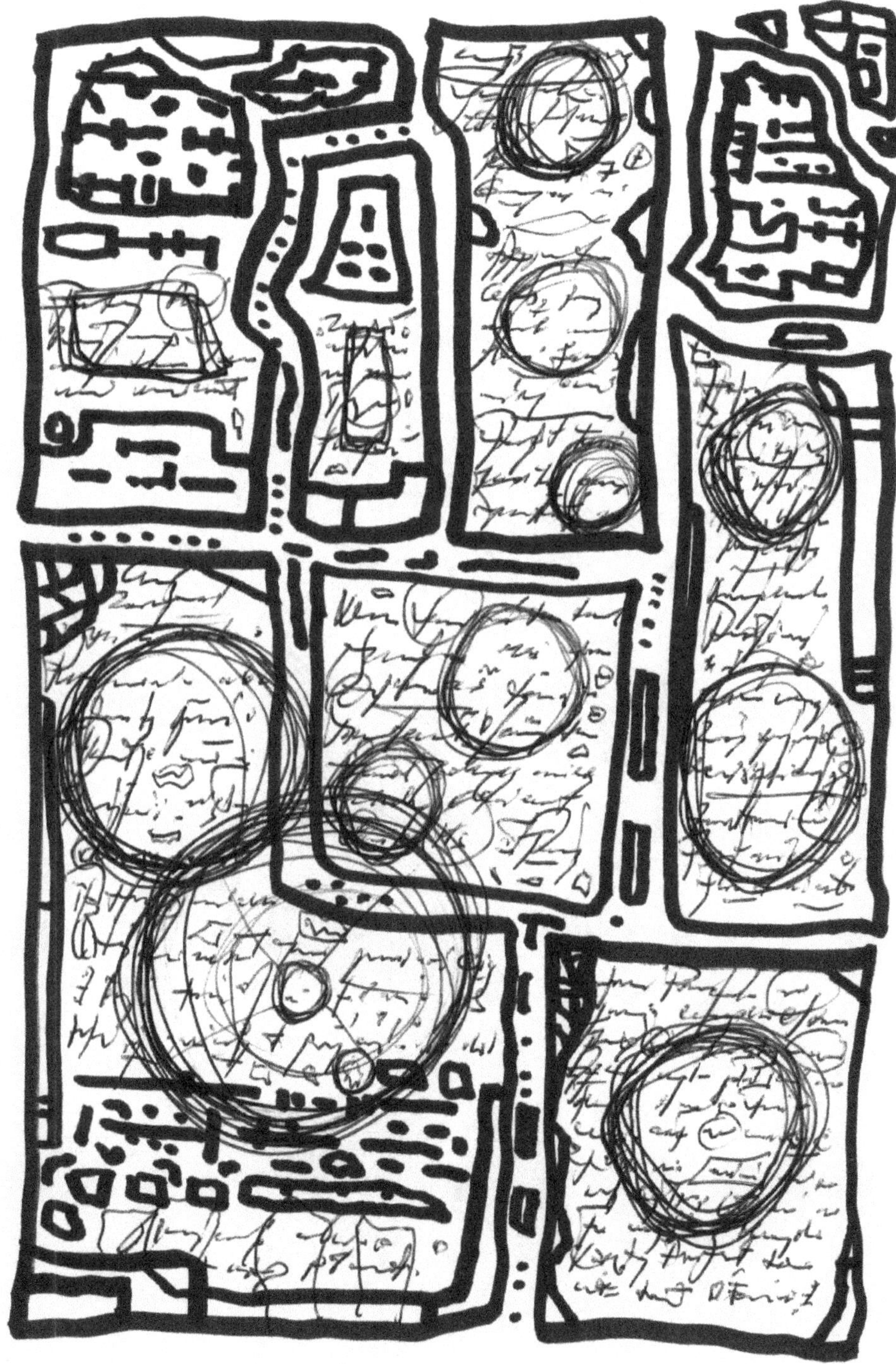

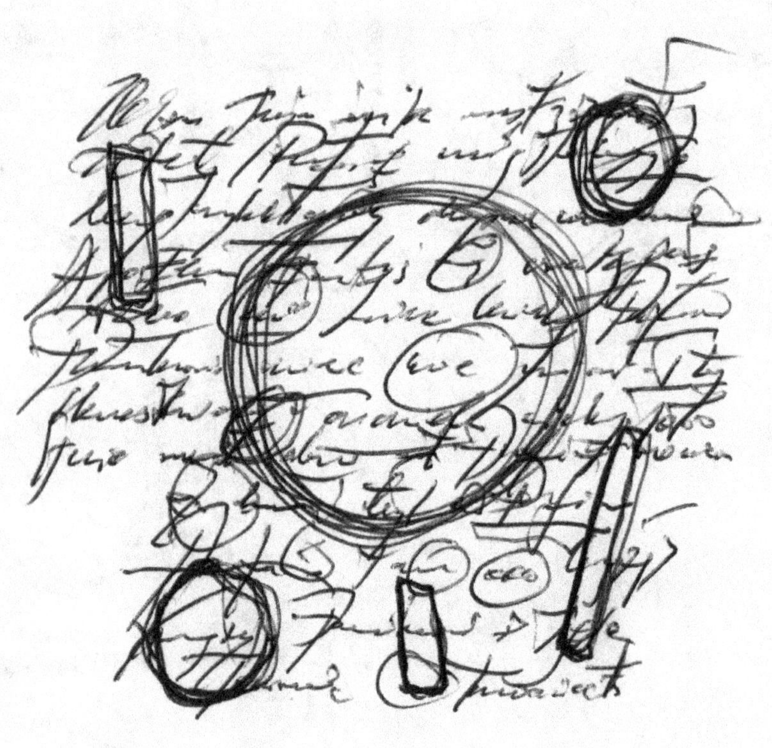

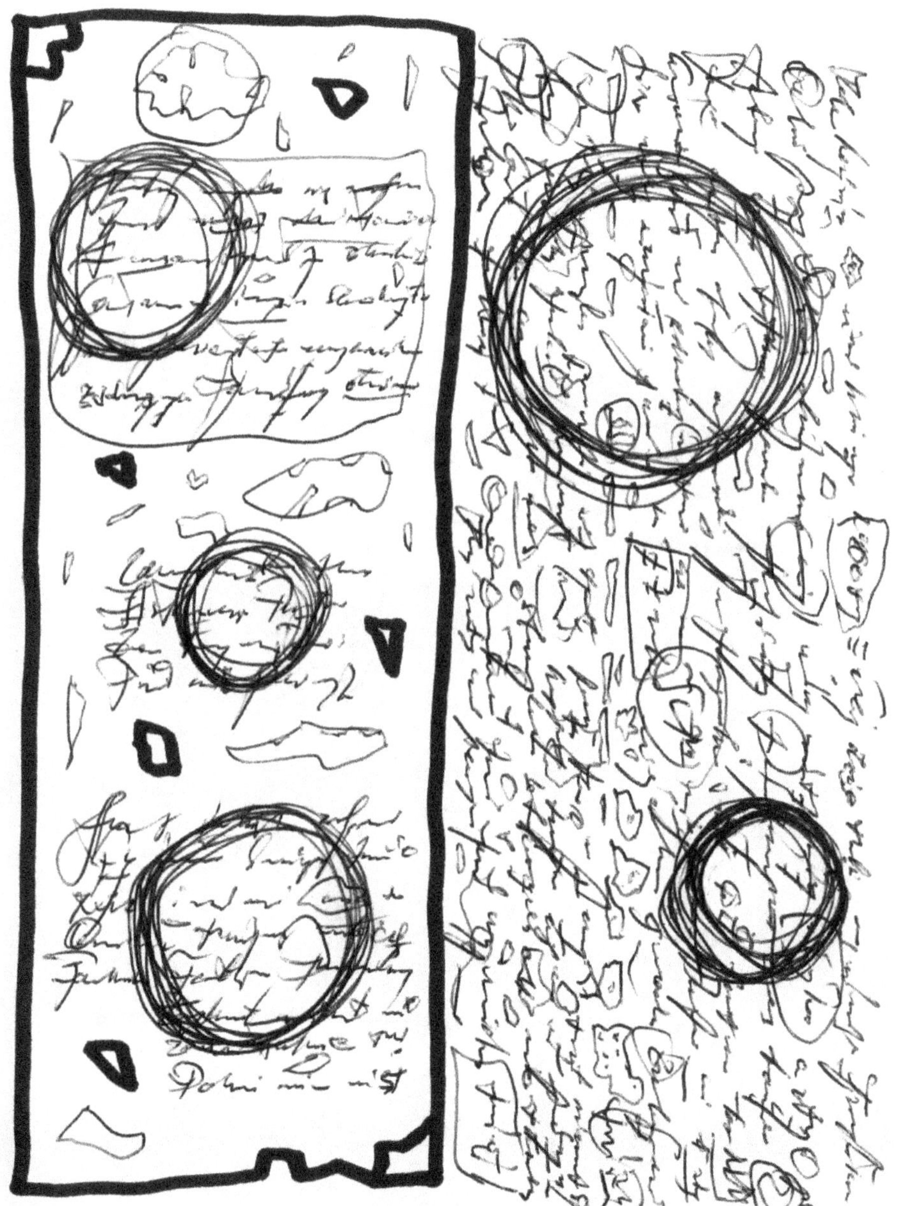

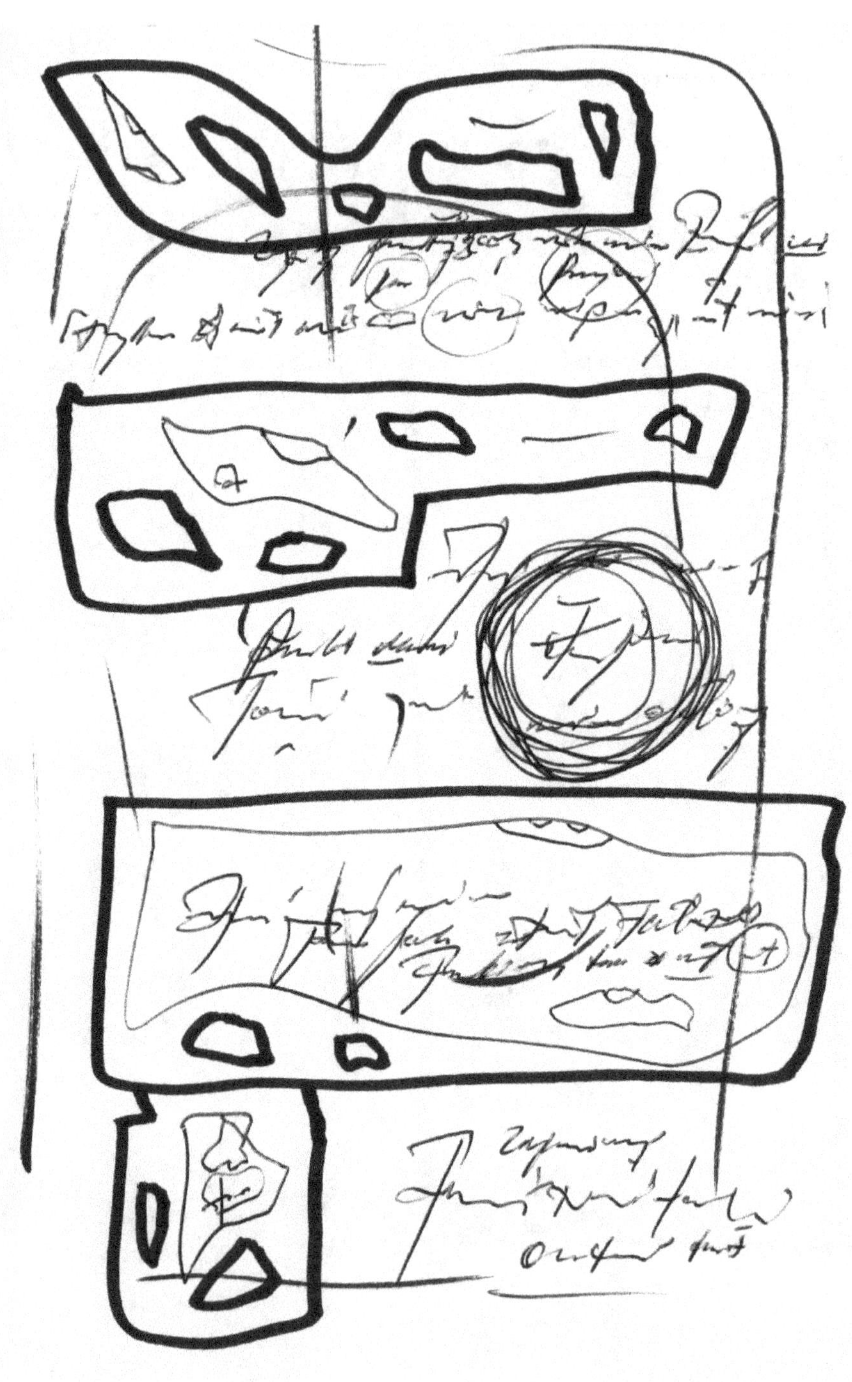

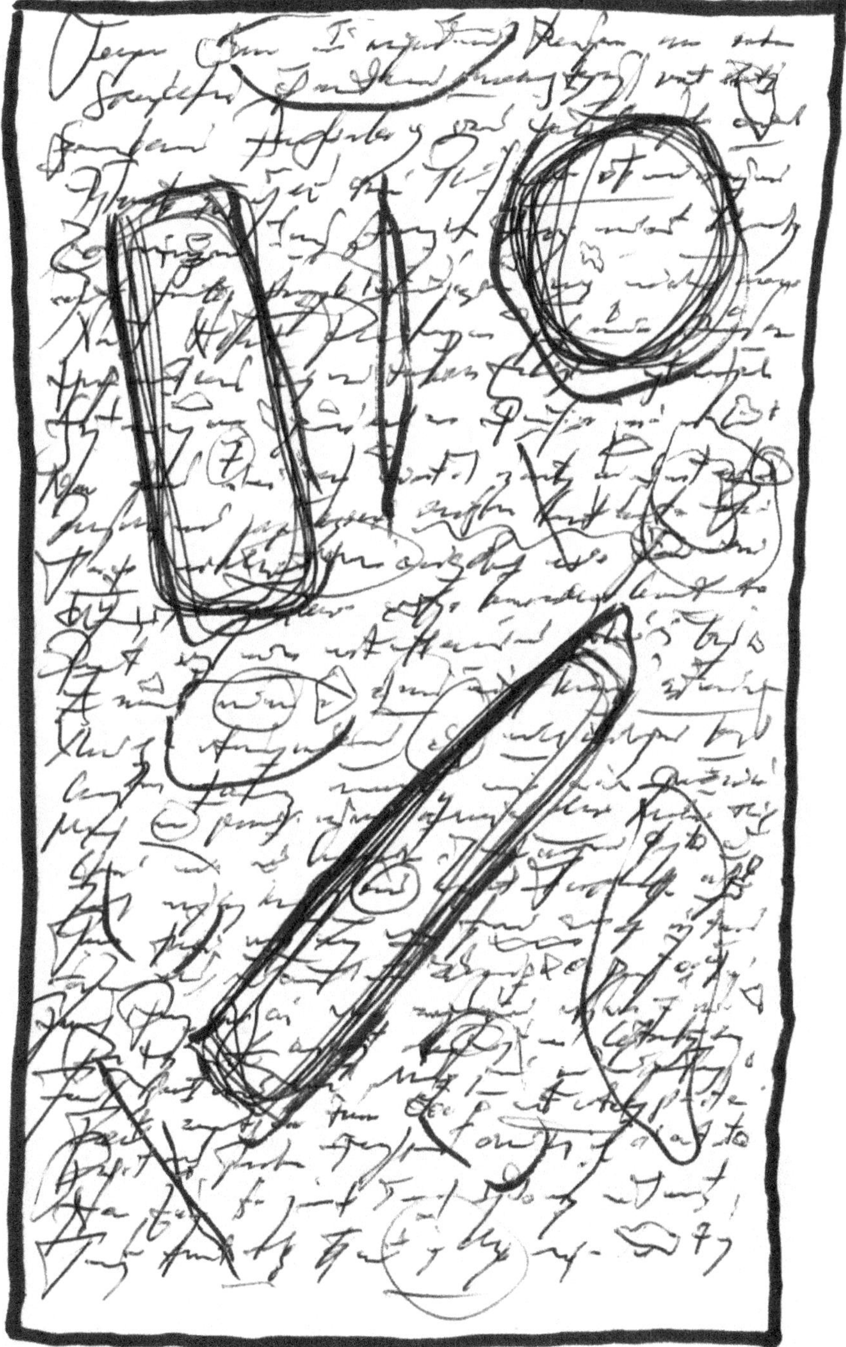

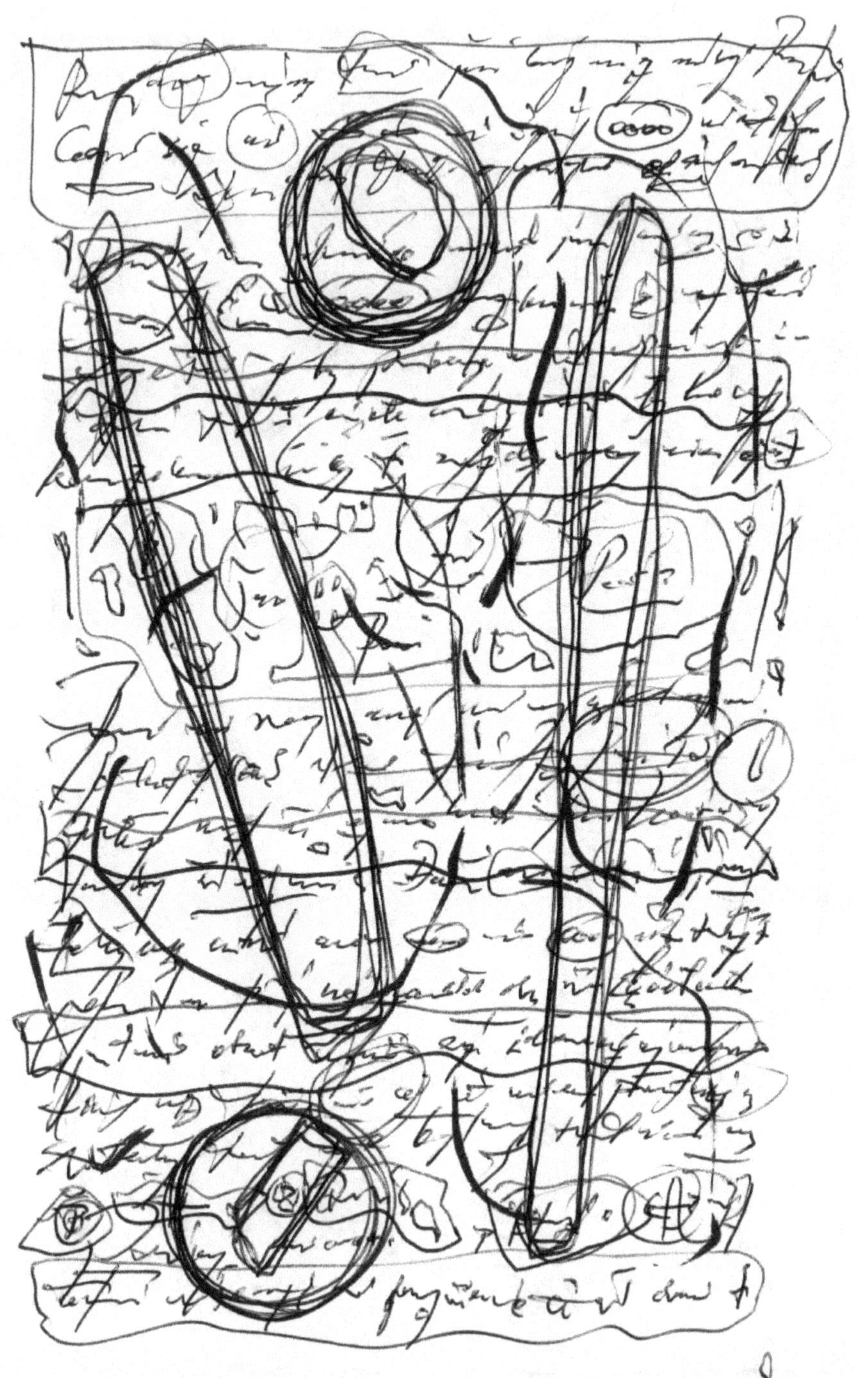

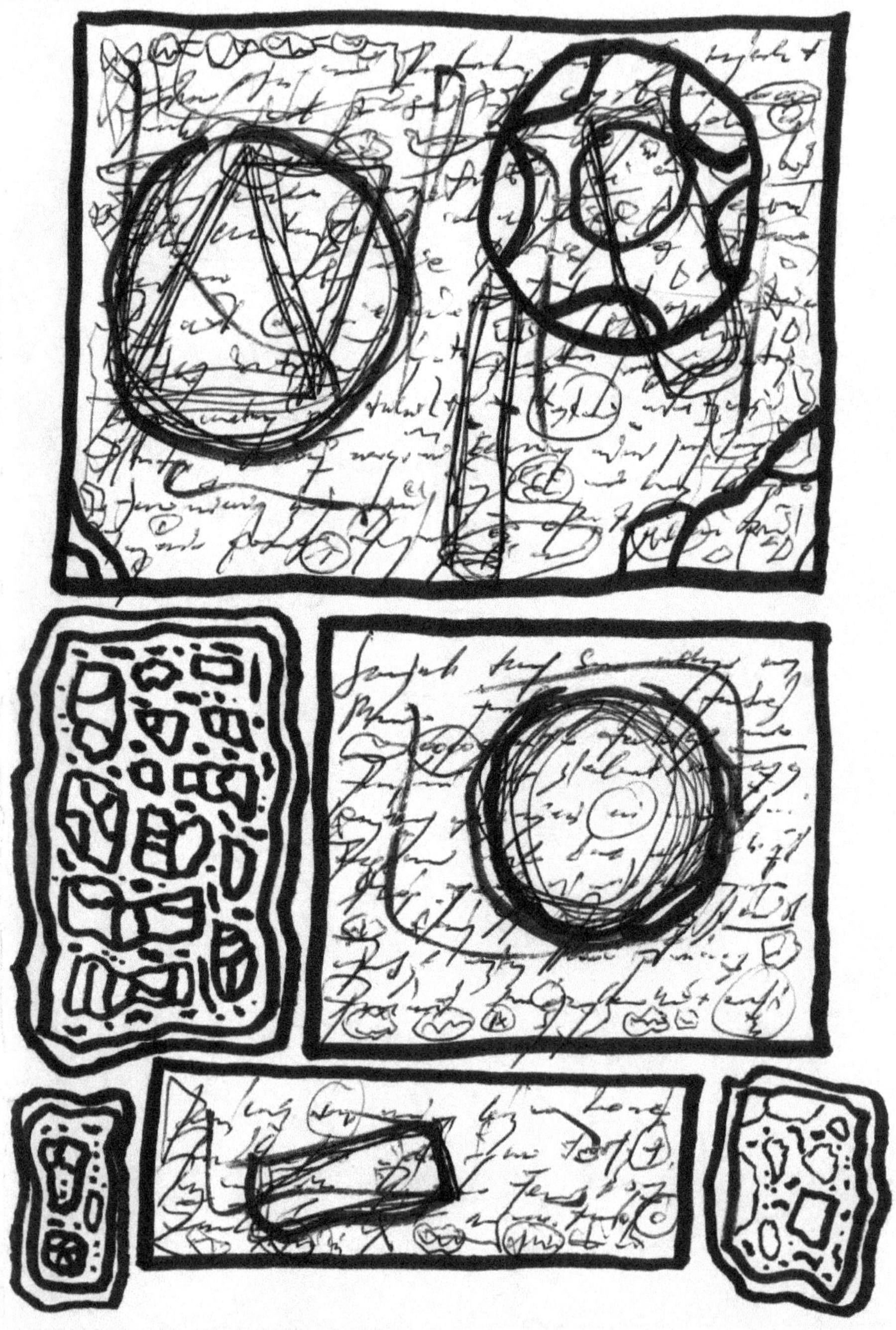

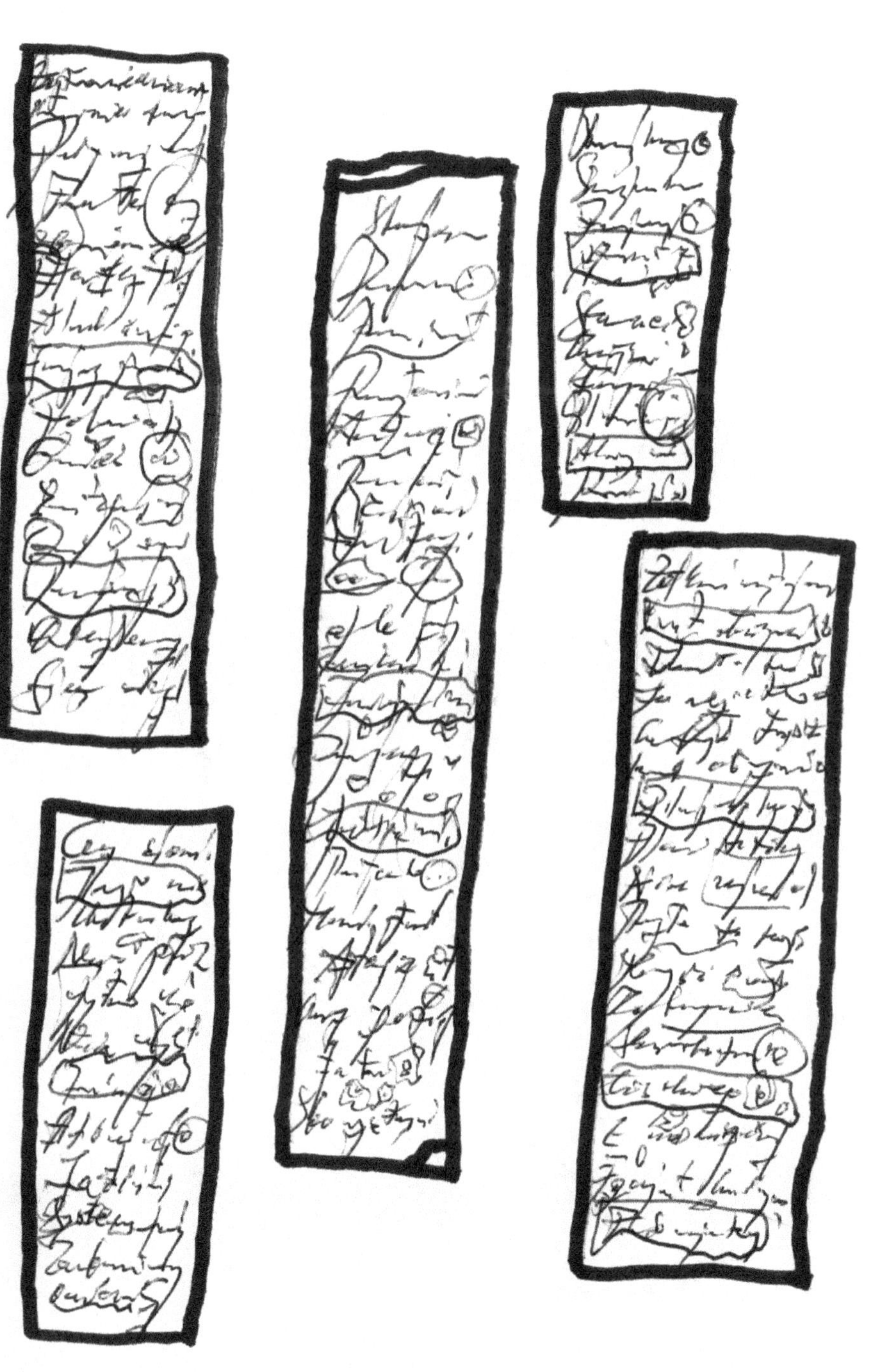

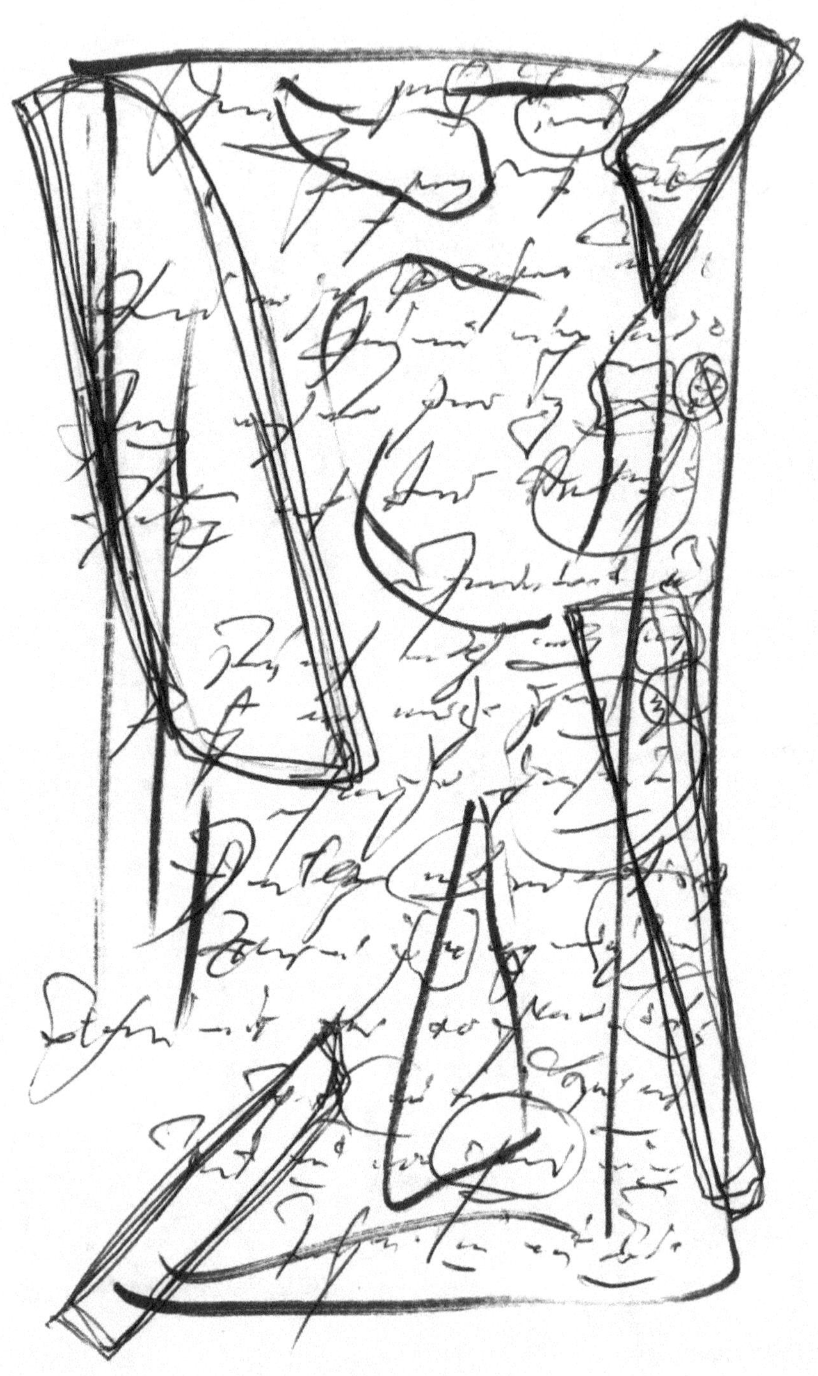

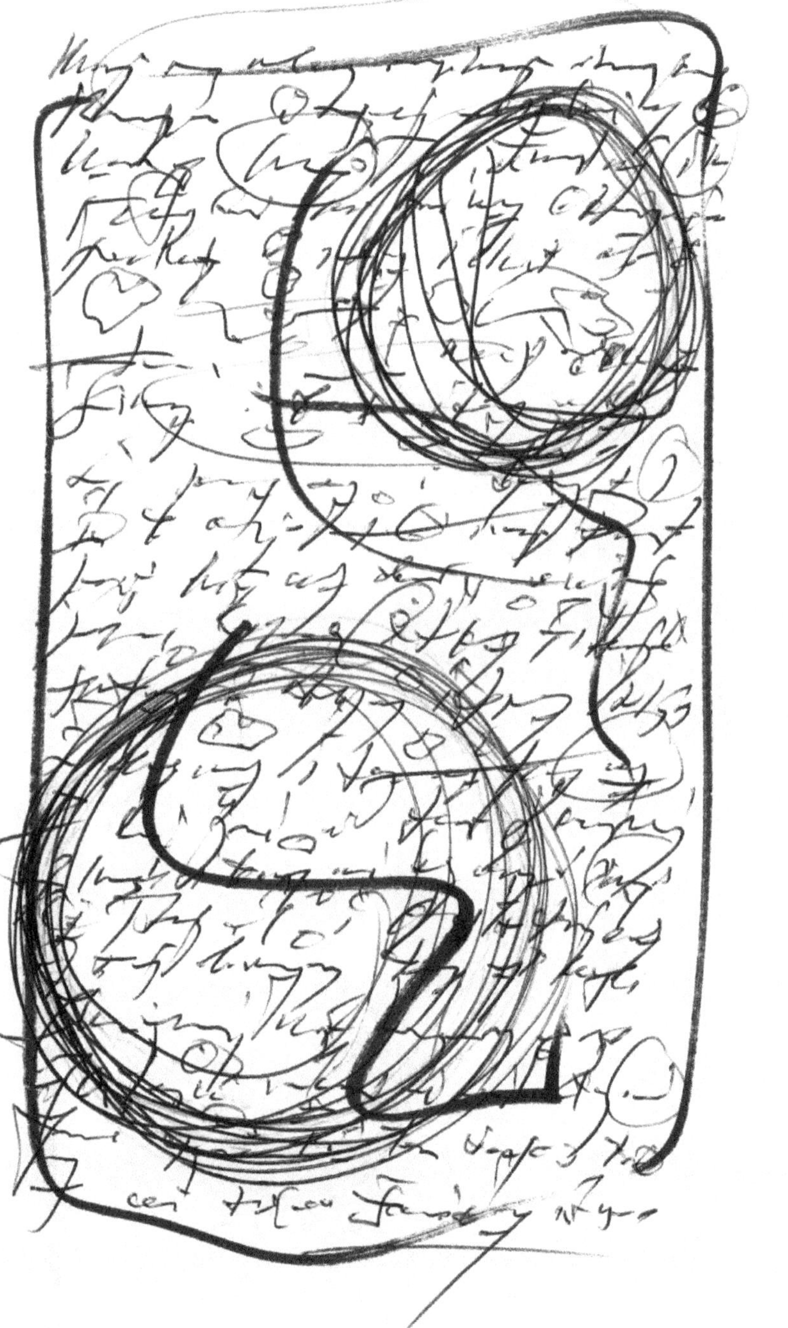

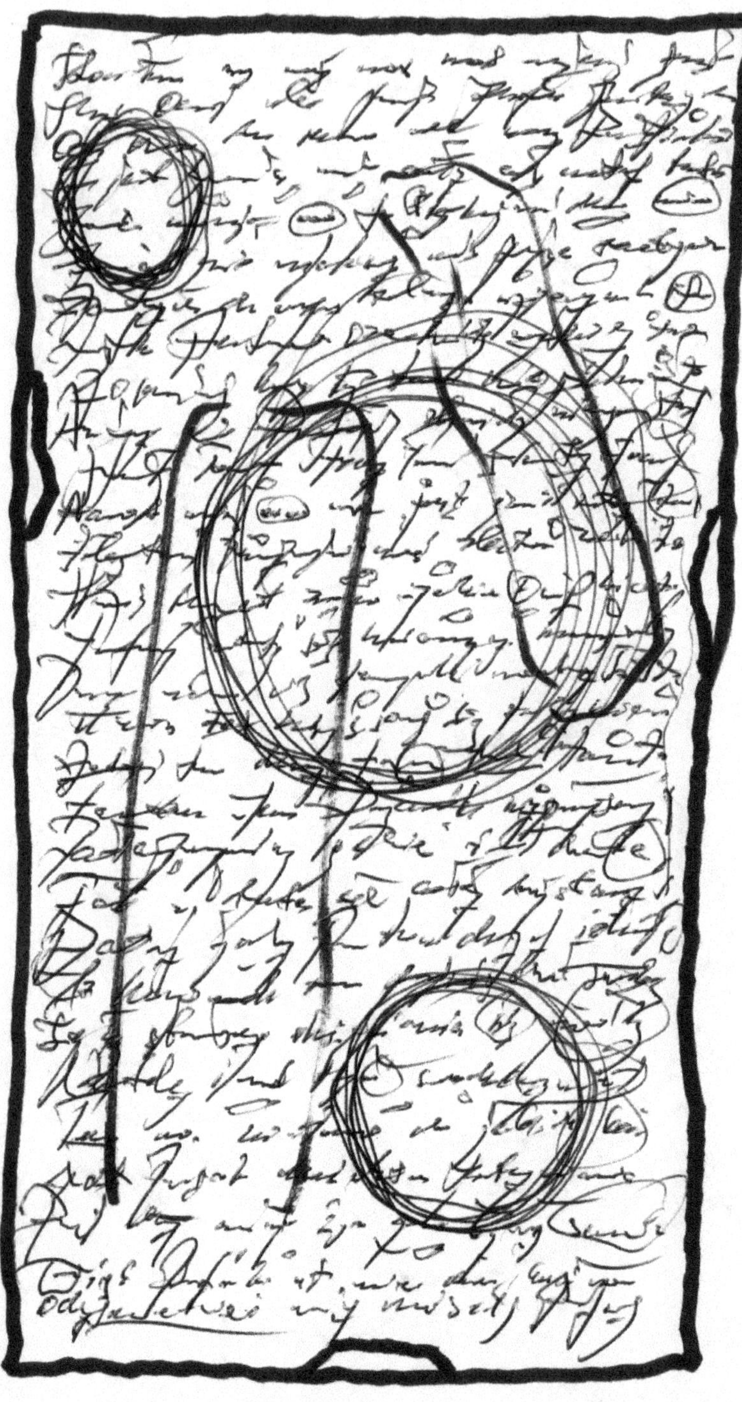

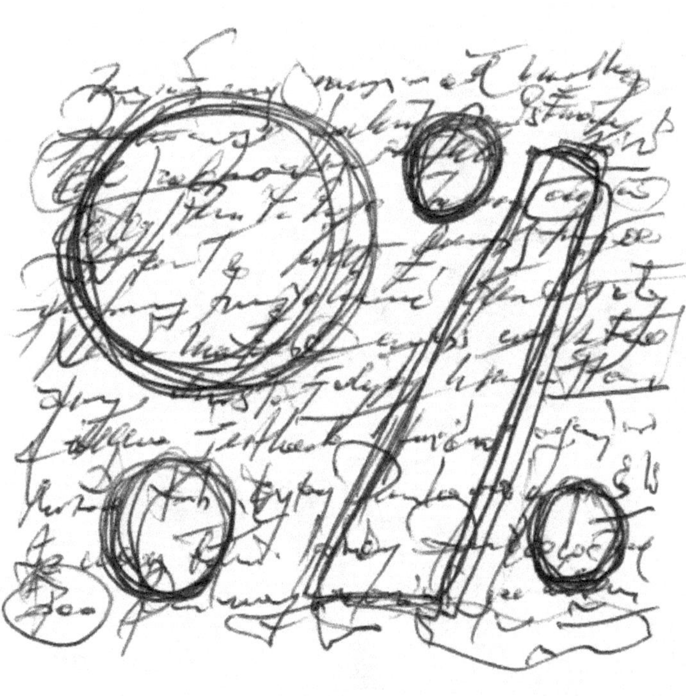

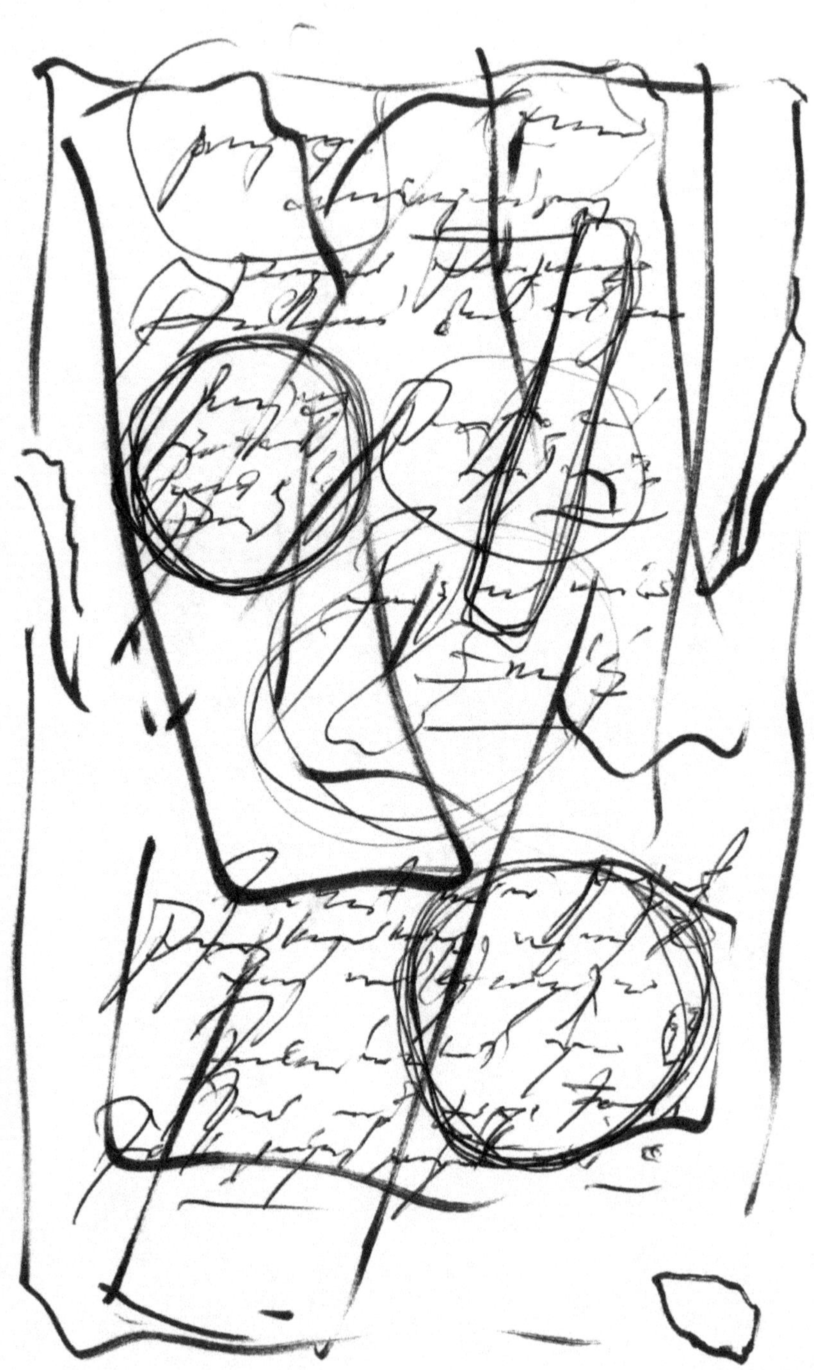

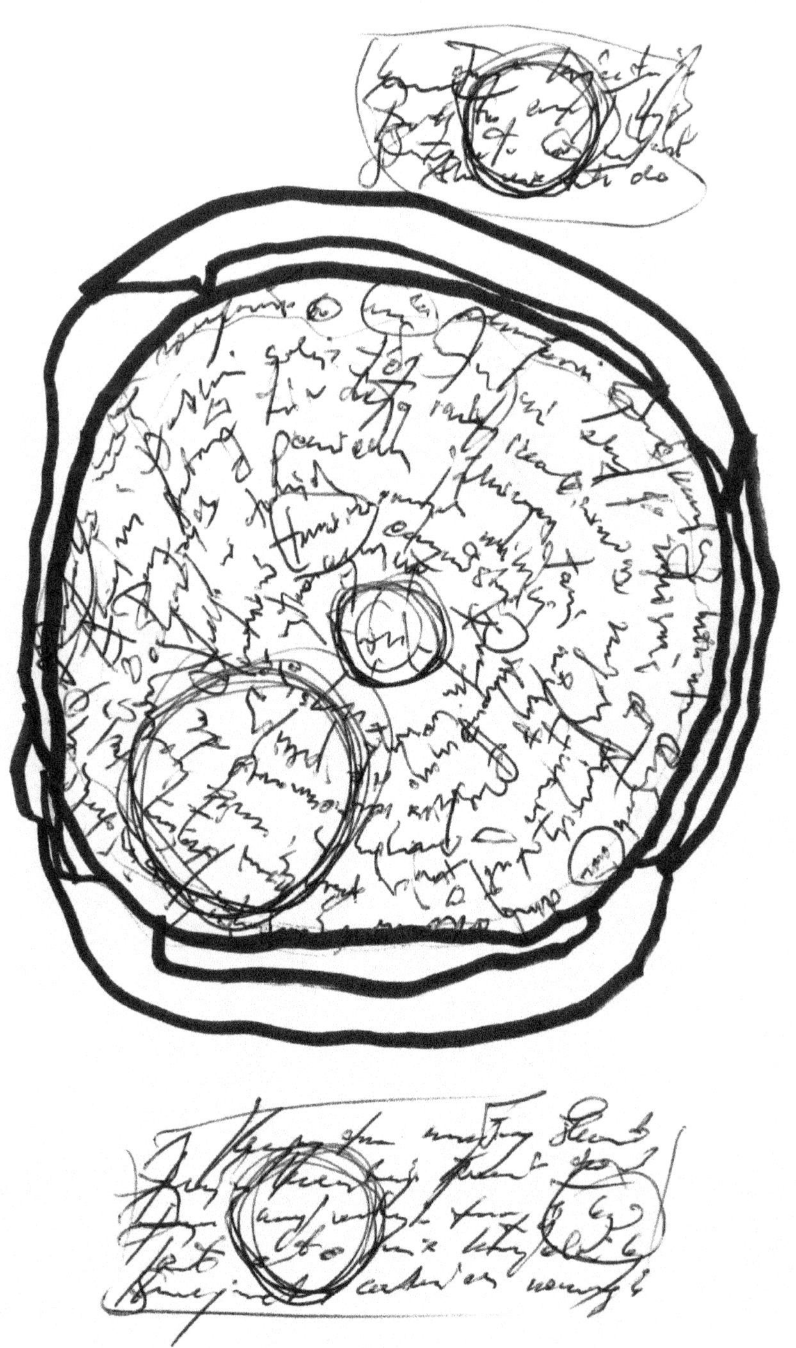

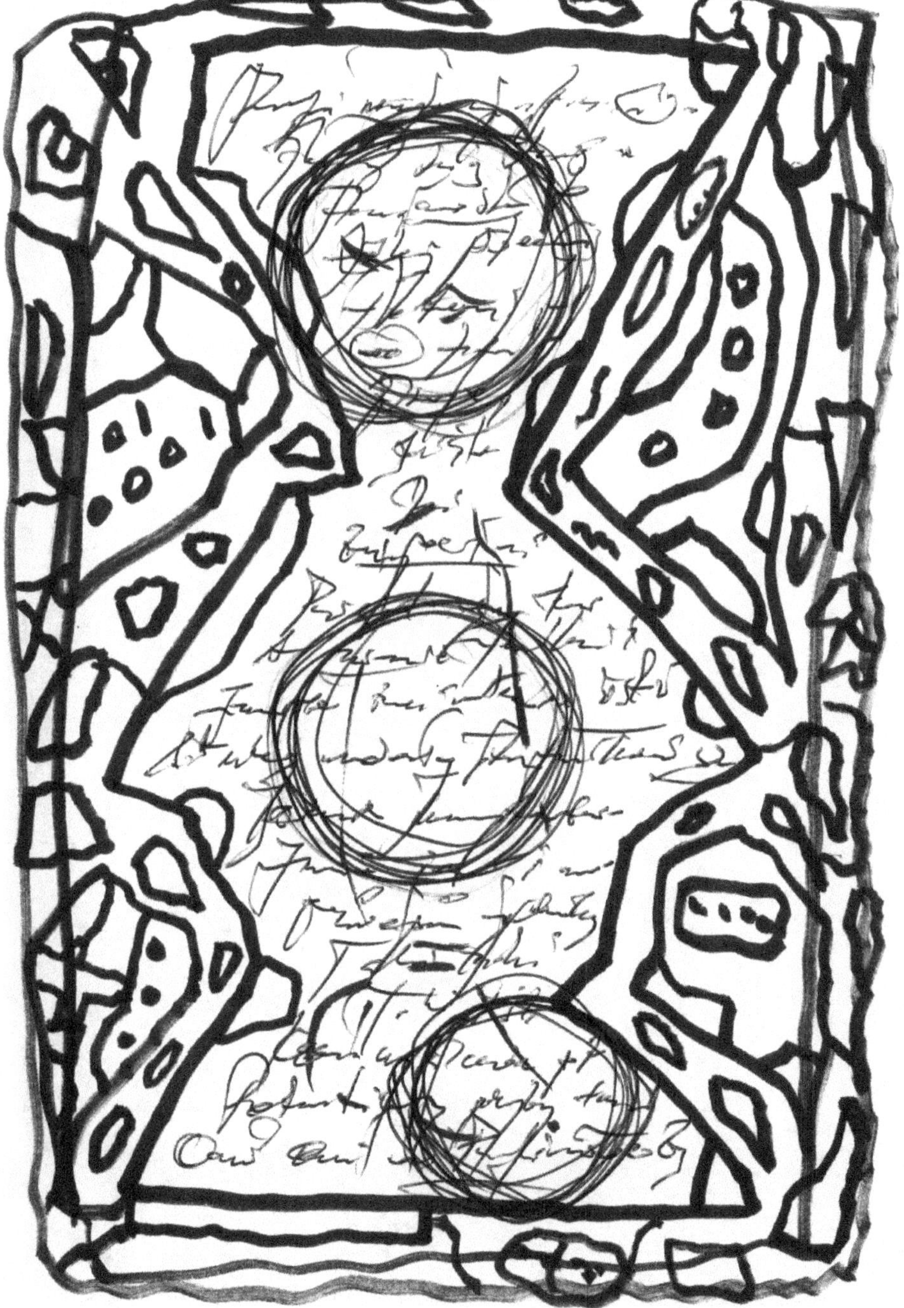

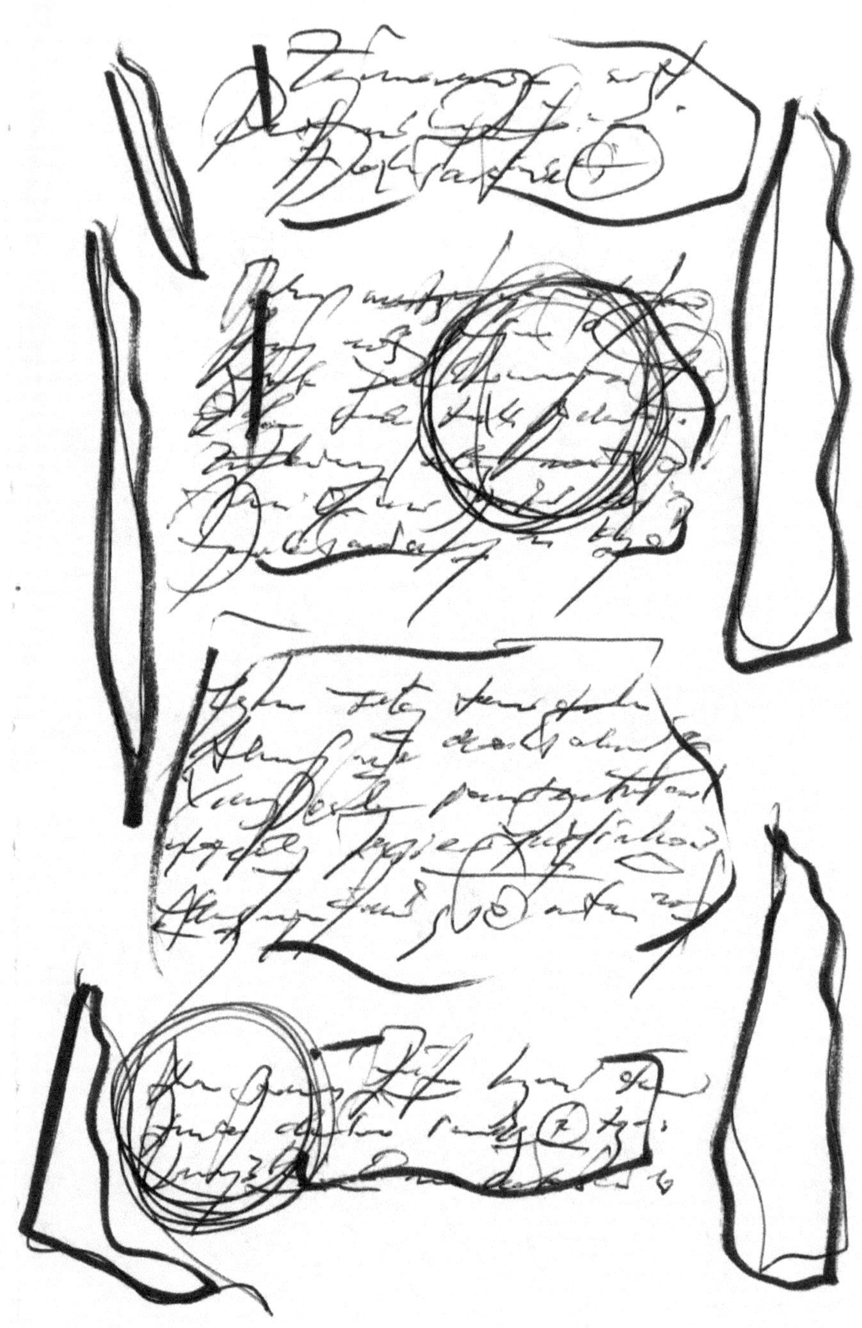

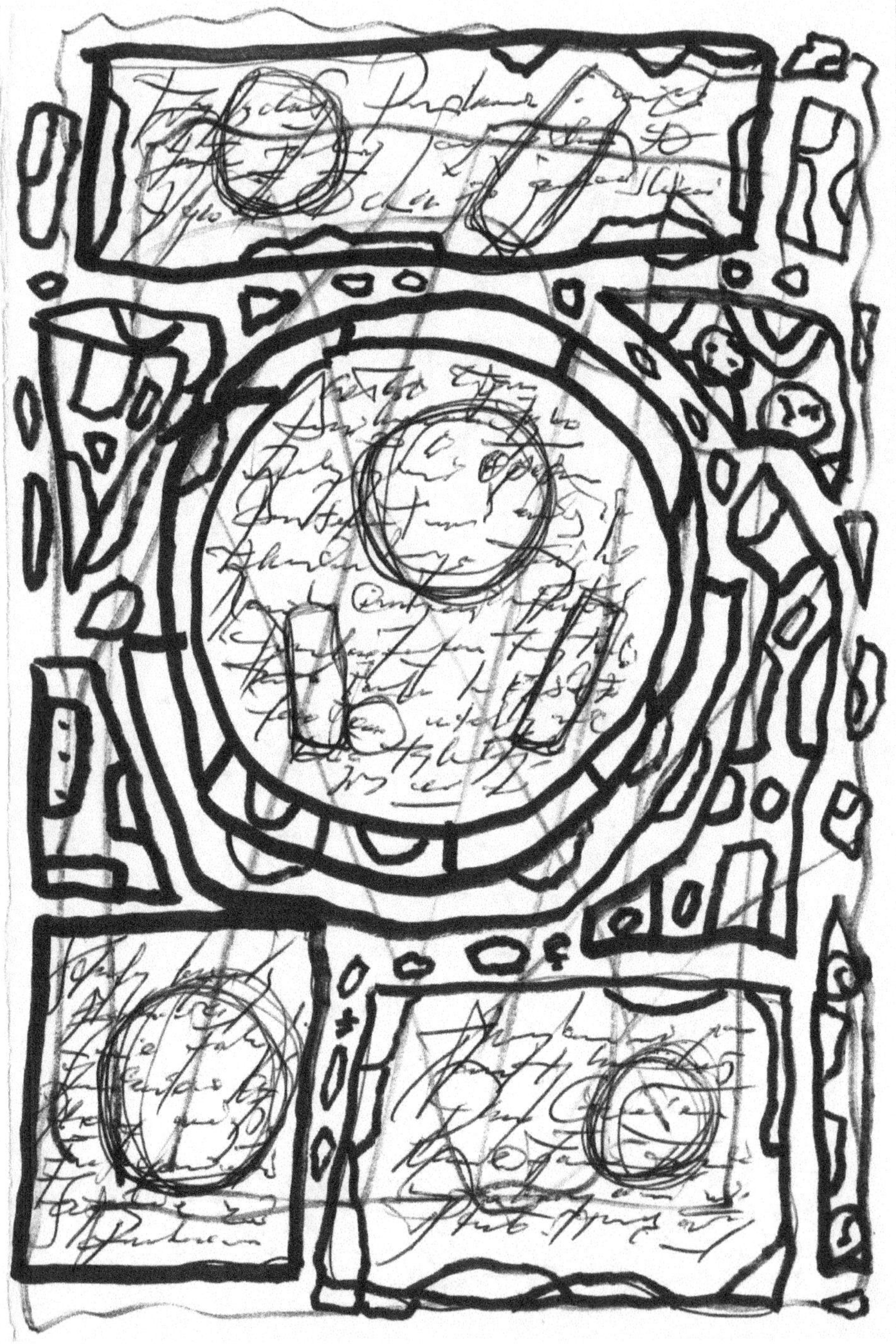

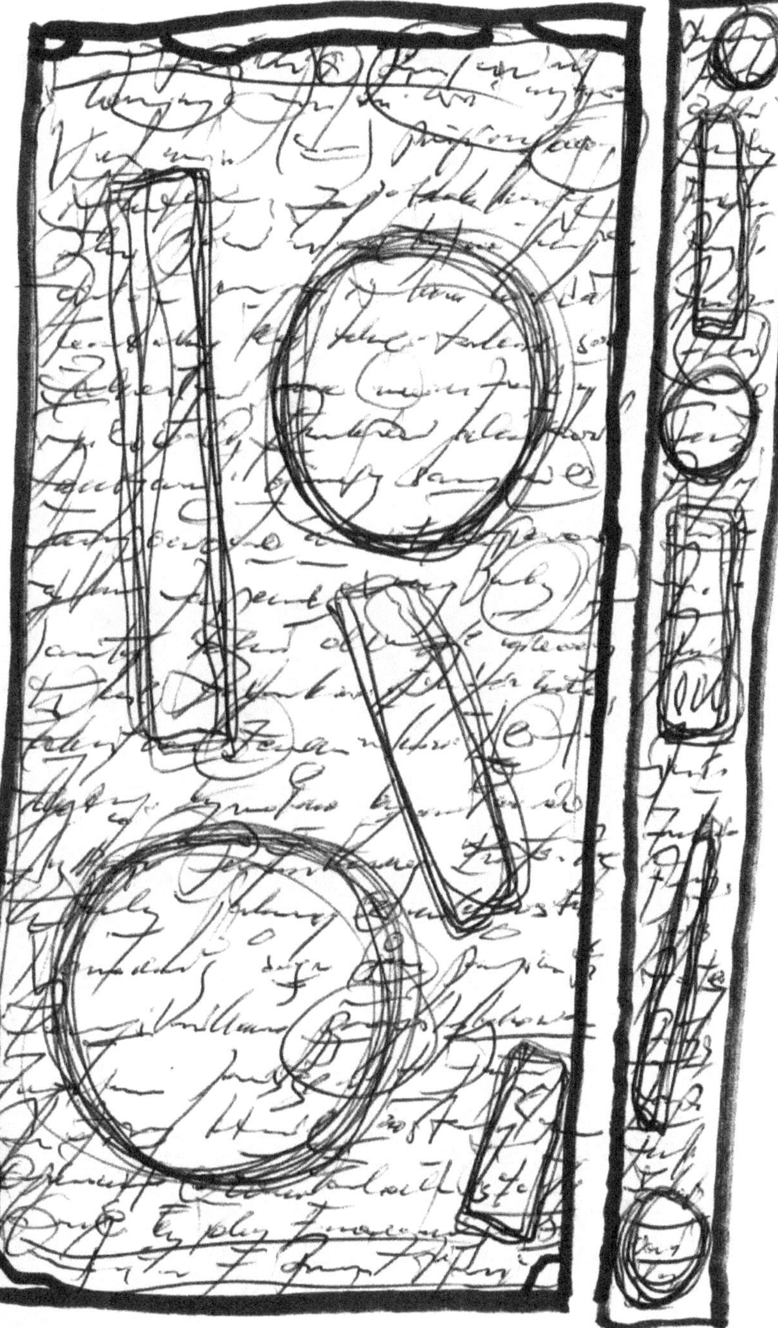

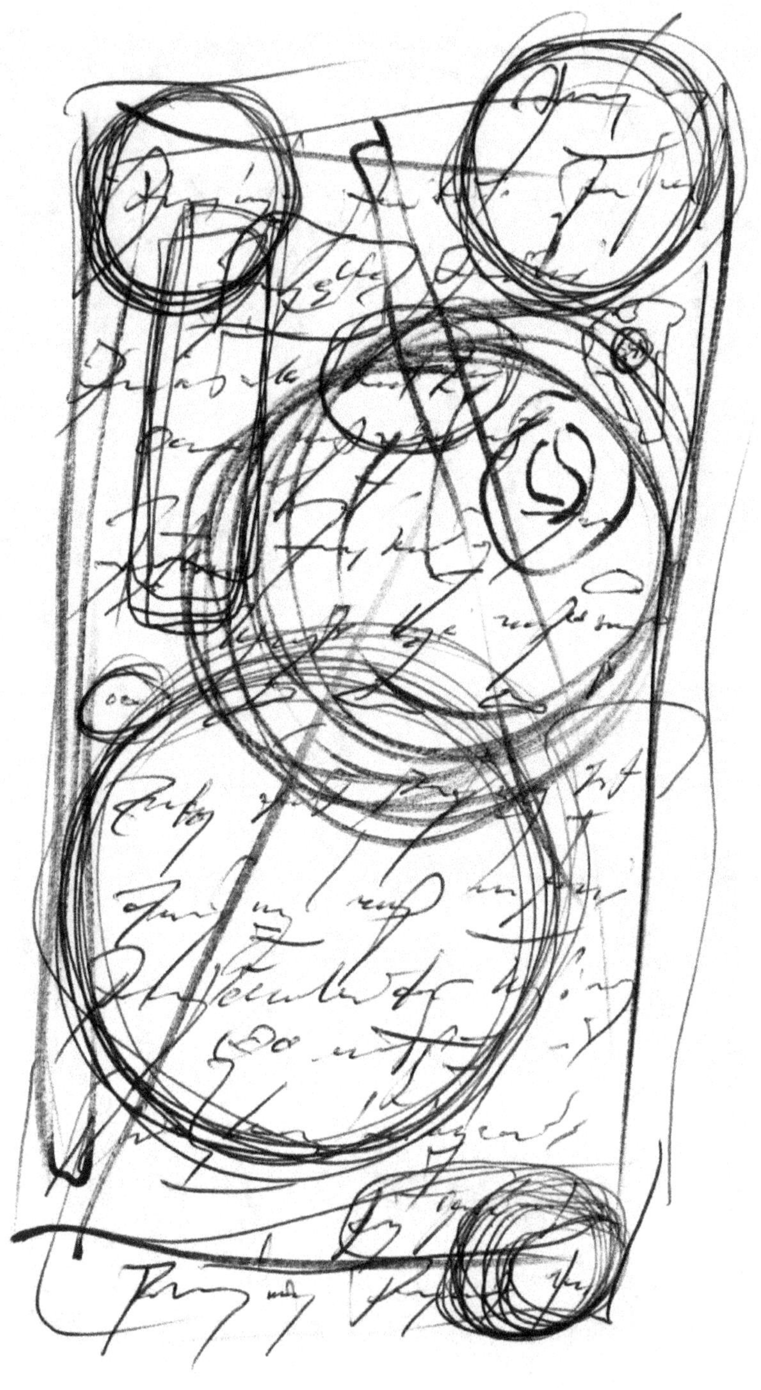

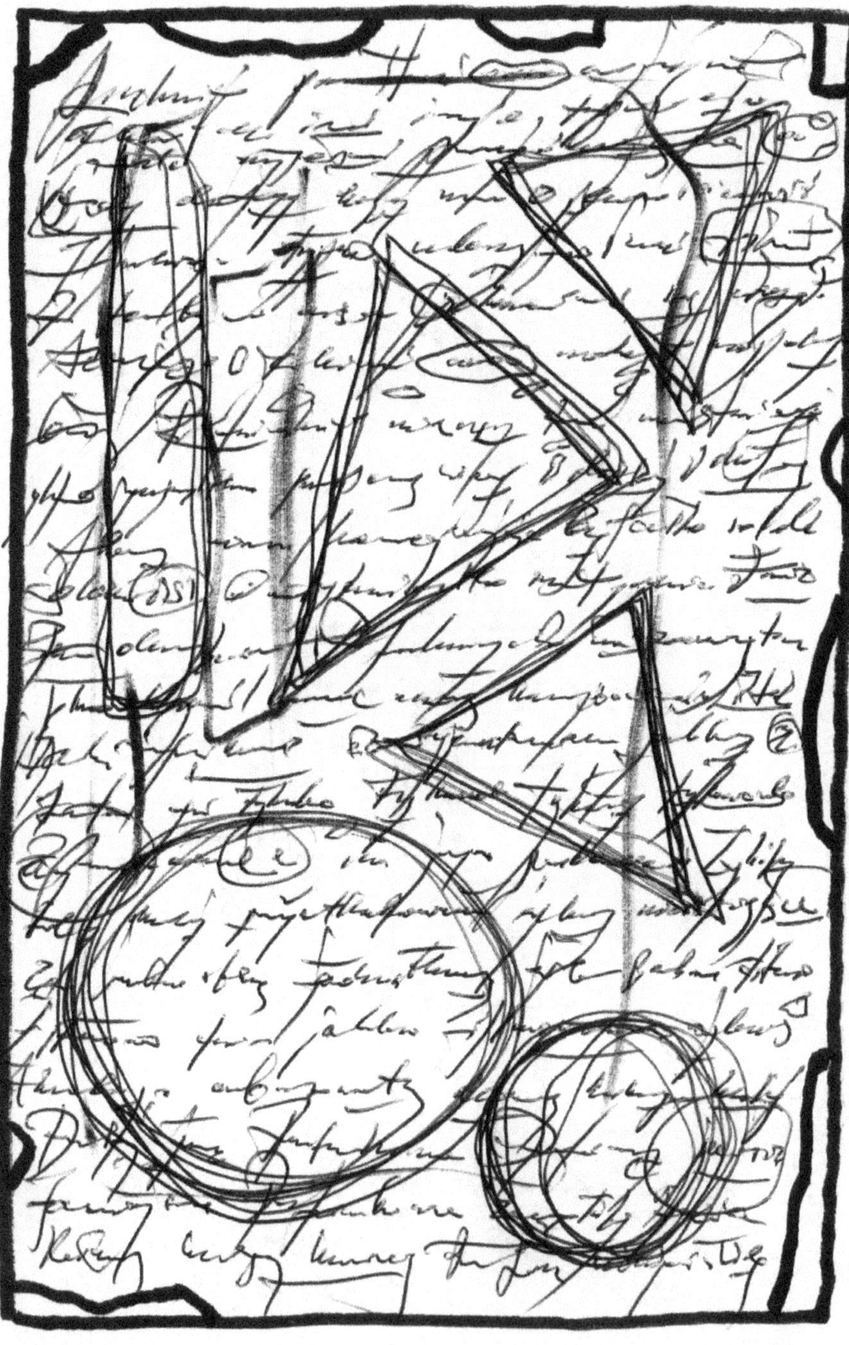

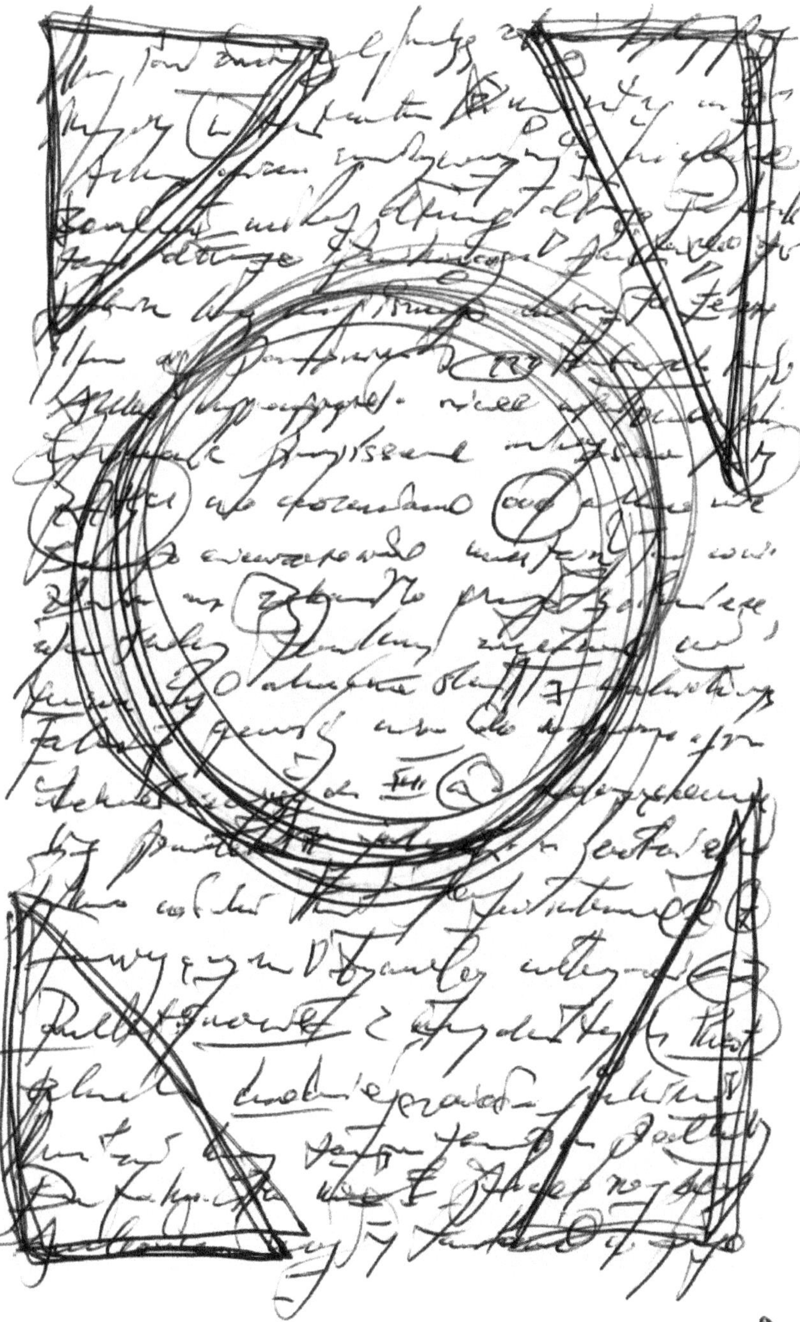

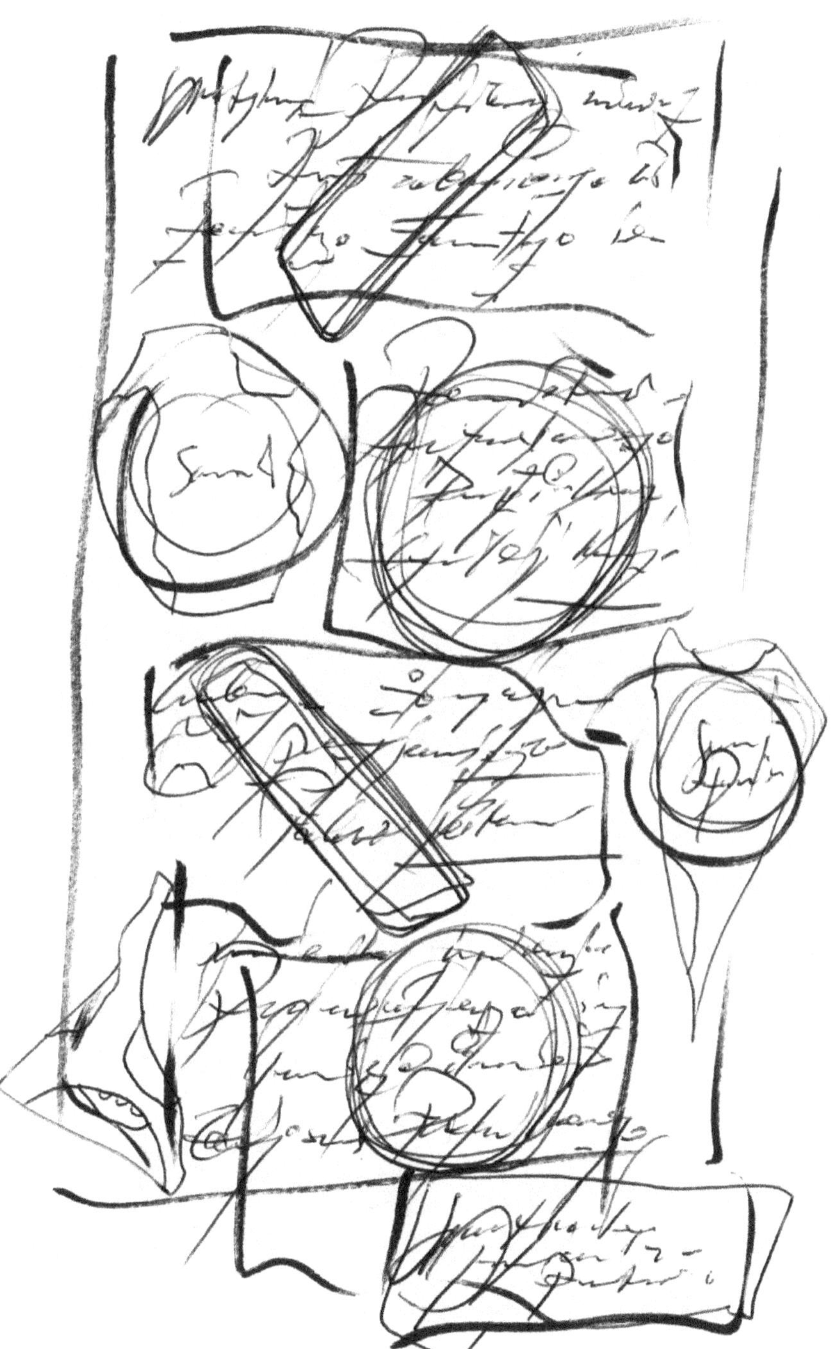

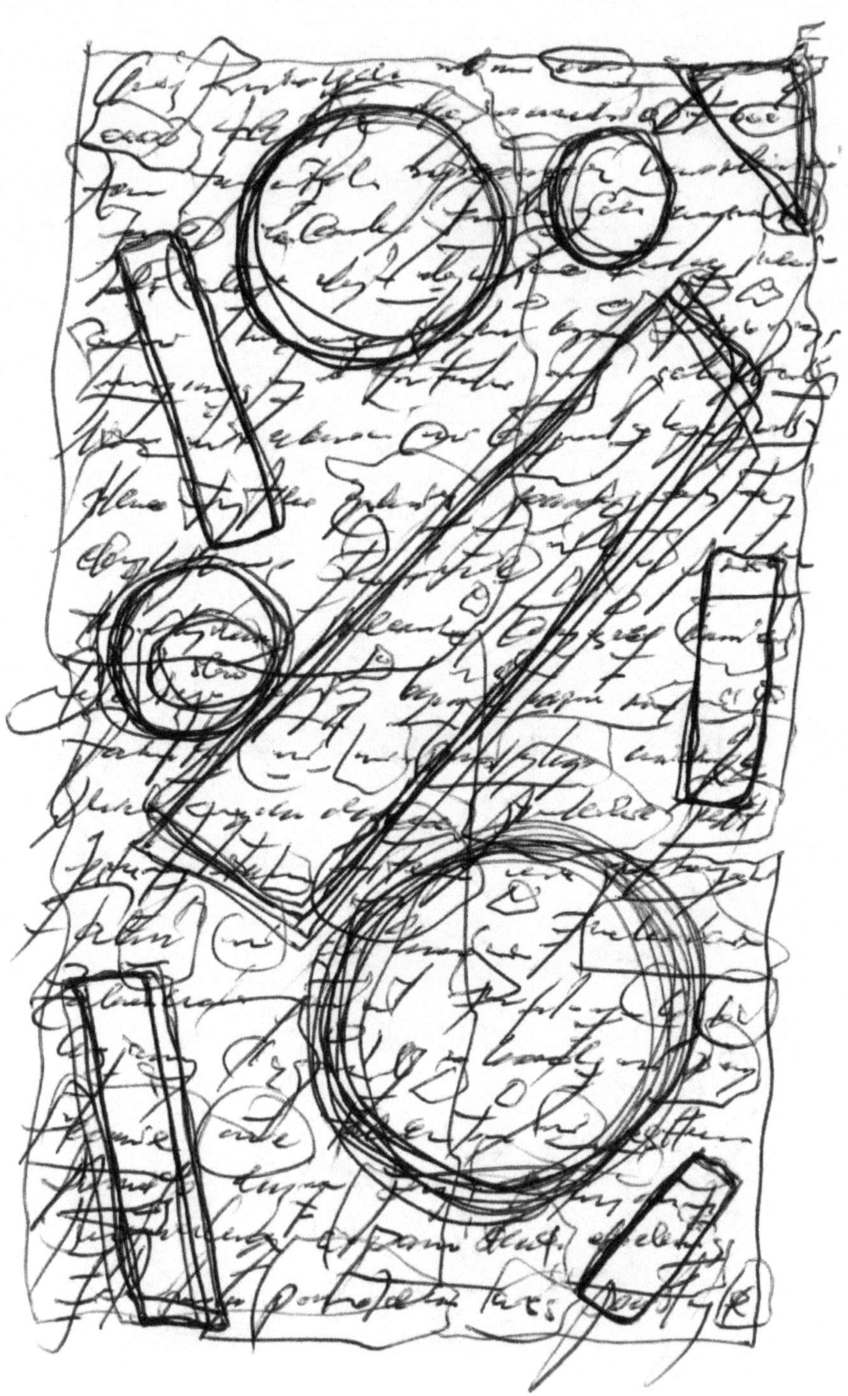

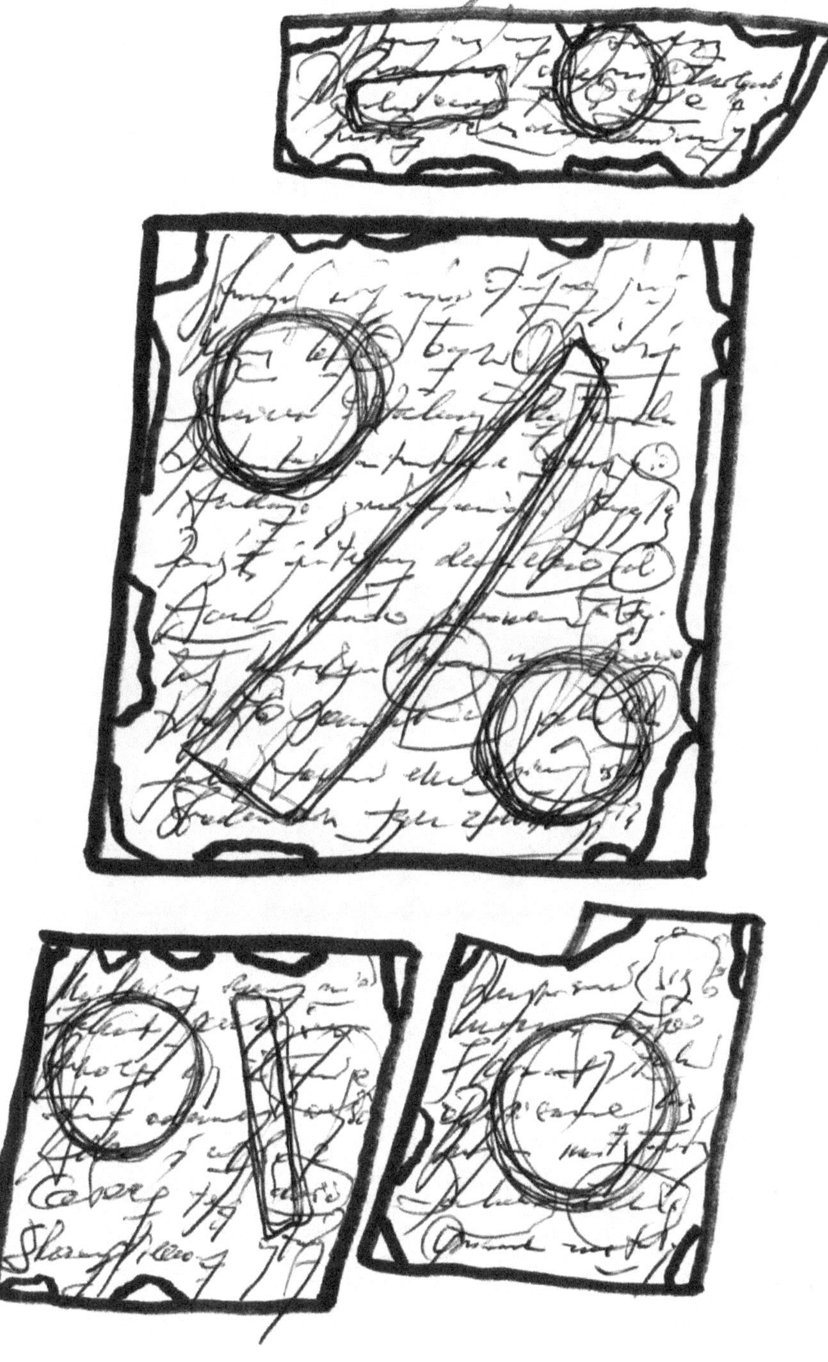

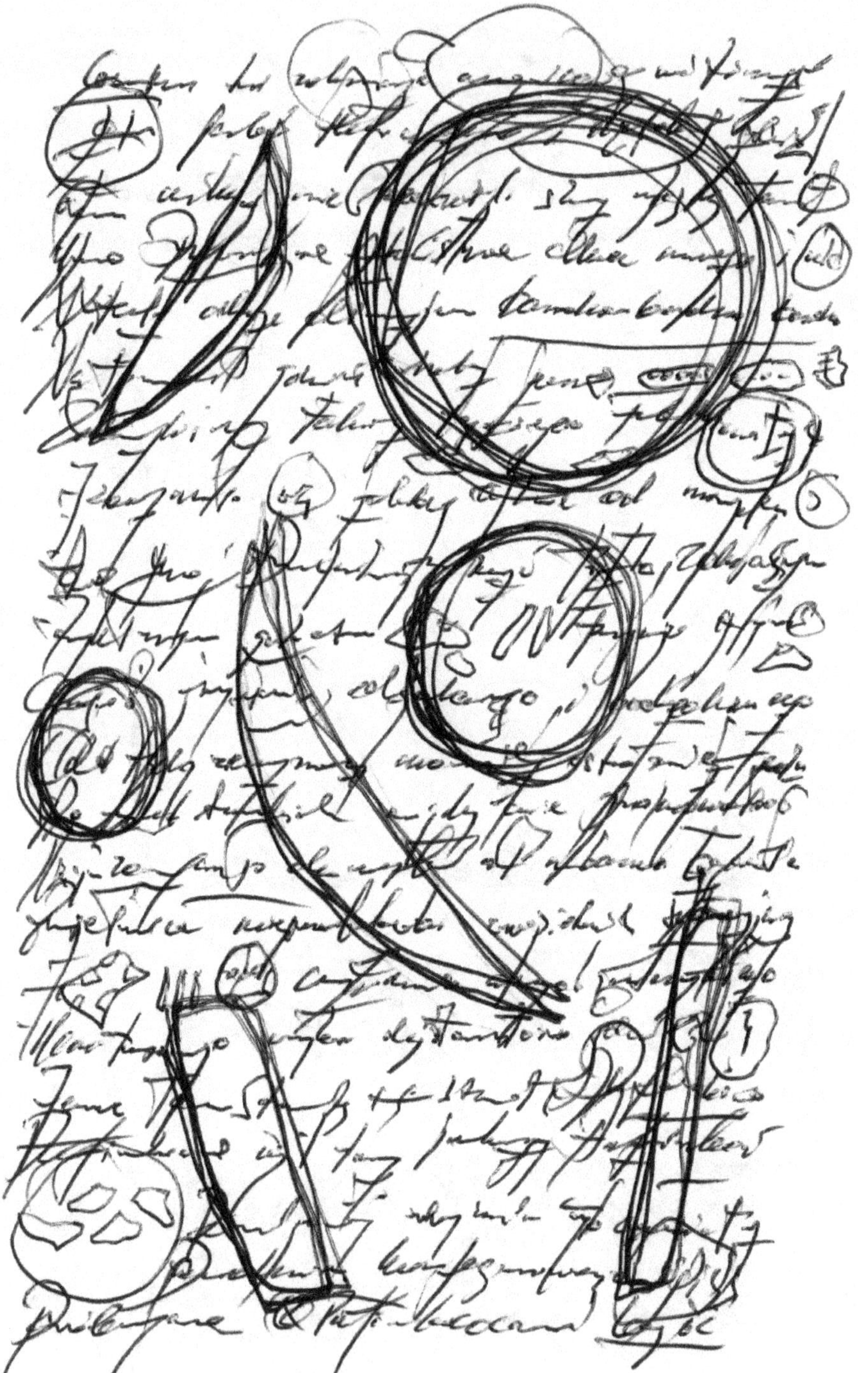

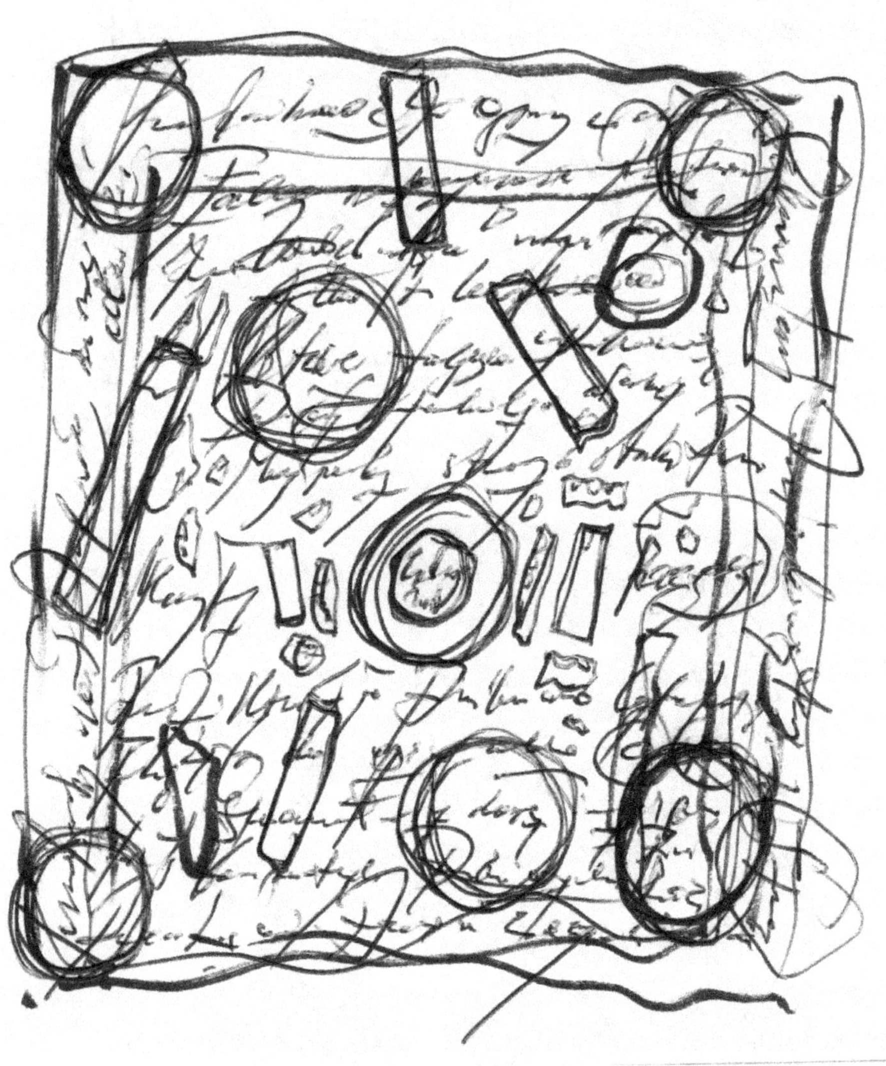

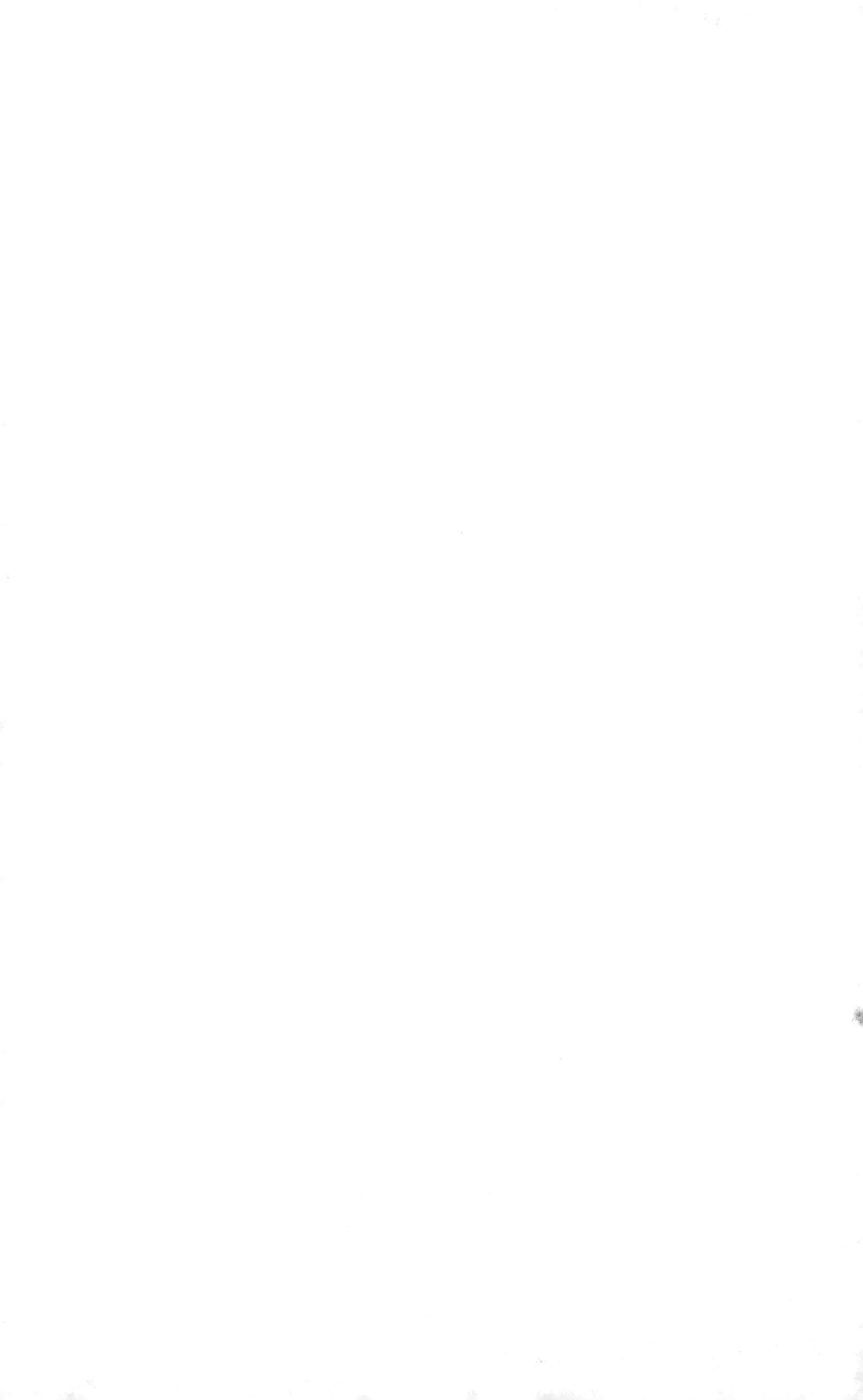

www.ingramcontent.com/pod-product-compliance
Lightning Source LLC
LaVergne TN
LVHW010544100826
845148LV00013B/2594

* 9 7 8 1 7 3 4 8 6 6 2 7 8 *